FRENCH AS THE COMMON LANGUAGE IN QUÉBEC
HISTORY, DEBATES AND POSITIONS

NEW PERSPECTIVES IN QUÉBEC STUDIES

A collection published by the Éditions Nota bene in cooperation with *Globe. Revue internationale d'études québécoises.*

The main objective of the collection "New Perspectives in Québec Studies" is to ensure a wider diffusion of scientific knowledge about Québec. Each volume contains the English translation of one or more articles previously published in French in *Globe. Revue internationale d'études québécoises.*

This collection is directed by Daniel Chartier.

Ian Lockerbie, Ines Molinaro,
Karim Larose, Leigh Oakes

French as the Common Language in Québec

History, Debates and Positions

With a Presentation by
Daniel Chartier

ÉDITIONS NOTA BENE/GLOBE
NEW PERSPECTIVES IN QUÉBEC STUDIES

These four articles were previously published in French under the titles :

Ian LOCKERBIE, « Le débat sur l'aménagement du français au Québec », *Globe. Revue internationale d'études québécoises*, vol. 6, n° 1, 2003, p. 125-149.

Ines MOLINARO, « Contexte et intégration. Les communautés allophones au Québec », *Globe. Revue internationale d'études québécoises*, vol. 2, n° 2, 1999, p. 101-124.

Karim LAROSE, « L'émergence du projet d'unilinguisme. Archéologie de la question linguistique québécoise », *Globe. Revue internationale d'études québécoises*, vol. 7, n° 2, 2004 p. 177-194.

Leigh OAKES, « Le français comme "langue publique commune" au Québec », *Globe. Revue internationale d'études québécoises*, vol. 7, n° 2, 2005, p. 155-176.

This book is published in cooperation with :

Globe. Revue internationale d'études québécoises
Département d'études littéraires
Université du Québec à Montréal
Case postale 8888, Succursale Centre-ville
Montréal (Québec) Canada H3C 3P8
www.revueglobe.uqam.ca
revueglobe@uqam.ca

The Editor wishes to thank Karine Cellard, Michel Lacroix
and Catherine Vaudry for their editorial support.

Globe. Revue internationale d'études québécoises,
acknowledges the financial support of the Canada Magazine
Fund of Heritage Canada for this promotion project.

"L'émergence du projet d'unilinguisme.
Archéologie de la question linguistique québécoise"
has been translated by Elaine Kennedy.

Cover : Typeface in Garaline,
created by Éric de Berranger (Montréal).
Cover designed by Jean-Olivier Noreau (Montréal).

Les Éditions Nota bene acknowledge the financial support
of the Canada Council for the Arts, the SODEC,
from the Government of Quebec, and of the Government
of Canada through the Book Publishing Industry
Development Program.

ISBN 2-89518-208-6

CONTENTS

PRESENTATION

Daniel Chartier

The French language in Québec, so aptly designated by the term "langagement"[1] coined by Lise Gauvin, cannot be understood without regard for the moral, ethical, social, political, historic, linguistic, literary and identity issues with which it is interwoven. The language defines the collective identity of Québec through its difference with the rest of North America, but also with France : "The

---

1. *Langagement. L'écrivain et la langue au Québec,* Montréal, Boréal, 2000. "Langagement" is a blend in French of "langue" or "language" and "engagement" or "commitment".

11

illusion of the language. Neither the same, nor another. ANOTHER IN THE SAME"[2] writes Régine Robin. The language has been and continues to serve as an instrument of social change (through the feminization of vocabulary and creation of new words), an area of commonality in diversity (through the concept of common public language), a formal literary playing ground (through Joual, the use of different registers and accents), an urban laboratory (through plurilingualism and language planning), and a political reserve which, beyond partisan and patriotic differences, still elicits profound public interest.

This volume features texts by four authors, who present and analyze the history of and positions taken on the French language as a social, political and identity-related tool. Ian Lockerbie (University of Stirling, Scotland)

---

2. *La Québécoite*, Montréal, XYZ éditeur, "Romanichels poche" series, 1993 [1983], p. 183.

looks at the "aménagement" of French in Québec, focusing on complex choices bound up with questions of norms, lexical variations and anglicisms, and reflecting on Québec's ambiguous relations with French spoken in France. Ines Molinaro (University of Cambridge, England) presents a remarkable synthesis of the language and identity-related policies promoted by the Québec and Canadian governments. She underscores the contradictions such policies create in the management of bilingualism and multilingualism. She observes how the language choices made by allophone immigrants in Québec influence the possibility of securing French as the common language spoken by the population. Karim Larose (Université Laval, Québec) traces the emergence of the concept of unilingualism in Québec, which took shape at the end of the 1950s and was responsible for a veritable social and political revolution, the epilogue to which would be the adoption in 1977 of the *Charter of the*

French Language. Finally, Leigh Oakes (University of London, England) questions whether it is possible to "de-ethnicize" a language entirely, as the concept of French as a common public language suggests, and seeks means of making French acceptable and attractive to immigrants settling in Québec.

THE DEBATE
ON L'AMÉNAGEMENT DU FRANÇAIS
IN QUÉBEC

Ian Lockerbie

The debate on what is called *l'aménage-ment du français*[1] in Québec might to an out-side observer seem a slightly arcane matter, of interest perhaps to some professional linguists and educationalists, but to few others. On the contrary, it is a topic that has generated a

---

1. The term *aménagement* is quite often used to include the wider phenomenon of language legislation. In this article it is used only in its restricted sense, referring to the aim of identifying a distinct form of Québec French with its own range of registers, including a standard register.

15

surprising degree of conflict, with regular outbursts of controversy in the national media. The reason for this is that the issues involved are closely connected to questions of national identity, and arise from the often difficult and turbulent history of Québec, which has affected its language just as much as its institutions.

The quarrel is between two broad schools of linguists, whom we may call for convenience the *conservatives* (with no derogatory implication) and the *aménagistes*. What concerns both camps is the issue of *la qualité de la langue*. There is complete agreement between them that French in Québec, as the public language of the nation, should be of the highest possible quality. Where the dispute occurs is in choosing the standard by which language quality should be judged. The conservatives see the norms of good French as deriving directly from France, and requiring little or no adaptation for North American users. The *aménagistes* believe, on the

16

contrary, that French in North America has distinctive features which should be given an important place within any definition of the norm.

There is nothing unusual in discussion of language standards. All language communities develop a shared understanding of what is to be considered as the norm of correct language and are guided by this in a variety of ways. The norm, for example, is duly transcribed into grammar books and language teaching material and becomes the basis of what is taught in schools. It also implicitly determines the content of dictionaries and similar reference works which offer language guidance to the public at large. What makes the situation in Québec unusual is the abnormal history of French in North America and the sensitive memories that this has left in the group consciousness.

The key factor here is, of course, the long domination of French by English following the Conquest of 1759. For a long period

French Canada was isolated from France and its language. The use of English frequently became a condition of employment for French Canadians, and even where this was not the case, the high profile of English in the general language environment had considerable repercussions on the quality of French in everyday use. Québec French became pervaded by English words, used in the workplace, in commerce and in social life, with consequential effects on grammar and pronunciation. The result was a considerable impoverishment of the language which provoked feelings of alienation and dispossession in French Canada[2]. This is why the rehabilitation of French became a major cultural imperative of the Quiet Revolution of the 1960s. For the new corrupted form of French that Québec had inherited was a mark of inferiority that had to be overcome by a public commitment to the

---

2. See the excellently chronicled history in Chantal BOUCHARD, *La langue et le nombril. Histoire d'une obsession québécoise*, Montreal, Fides, 1998.

highest standards of language use. Correct French, "pure" French, became something to which every citizen should aspire as a condition of personal and national self-respect: *Bien parler, c'est se respecter.*

There is no doubt that these language aspirations have been largely achieved. Modern Québec is an upwardly mobile, very progressive society, and French as its public language has developed in pace with this process. This is not to say that language issues have ceased to be a preoccupation of Québec society, as the recent meetings (in 2001) of the *Commission des États Généraux de la Langue* have demonstrated. There are still many preoccupations with the pressures on French in a subcontinent which is overwhelmingly English-speaking. But in terms of the quality of the language, the problems faced now by Québec are no longer those of an abnormal linguistic situation, but rather those arising from social factors (*décrochage scolaire*, the integration of immigrants, etc.) which also occur in France and many other modern societies. The language encountered in every sphere of public activity is indisputably a standard form of French which any user of French as a world language will recognize without difficulty. This is what leads Chantal Bouchard to the relatively optimistic conclusion that, after 150 years of trauma, Québec society is at last overcoming its *insécurité linguistique* and feels relatively secure in its status as a French speaking nation[3].

Nevertheless, it is not an exaggeration to say that some sectors of public opinion remain haunted by the memory of the dark ages of linguistic degradation and that this colors their whole attitude towards the language. Even in the year in which Bouchard's book was published, a fierce confrontation broke out over the publication of the *Dictionnaire historique du français québécois*, a book which to the innocent outside observer would seem

---

3. *Ibid.*

to be an admirable work of scholarship, but which, by conferring academic legitimacy on the Québec variety of French, triggered certain internal phobias. Equally, in normal everyday reading of the Québec press, it would be unusual, in any twelve month period, not to find a crop of polemical articles protesting about allegedly deplorable standards of language use in every area of Québec life. The inevitable villain in such protests is the popular form of speech known as *le joual*, which has become the shorthand term by which the Québec variety of French in general is demonized[4].

---

4. See Ian LOCKERBIE, "The place of vernacular languages in the cultural identities of Québec and Scotland", *Québec and Scotland : an Evolving Comparison*, Edinburgh, University of Edinburgh, 2003. That article deals with the whole question of *le joual* and the stigmatized popular registers of the language, which underlie and cast a baleful shadow over the work of the *aménagistes*. These matters are closely related to the present work but, to avoid duplication, are only briefly referred to here.

The conservative position on language quality is to some extent marked by the tendency to consider any local usage as linguistically inferior. While not rejecting Québec French totally, it sees its proper domain as being essentially the informal registers of popular, and mainly spoken, language. But for all public situations requiring serious, sophisticated and dignified use of language, only Standard French (SF)[5], the one internationally recognized and respected variety, is acceptable.

---

5. SF as used in this article is to be understood as the educated form of French spoken and written in France. The term *le français international* is often used in this sense, but this term is misleading in its implication that there is a standard form of French common to all French speakers *which is distinct from that used in France*. This is not the case, and the term thus obscures all the issues involved in the concept of language variety. A better set of descriptive terms will hopefully emerge when these issues become better known. What is especially missing is a term to refer to the common core of French vocabulary, i.e. the large stock of "neutral" words used by all French speakers : *le français commun*, as suggested by Pierre MARTEL and Hélène CAJOLET-LAGANIÈRE seems possible (*Le français québécois. Usages,*

Perhaps it is true that, at a certain historical stage, it was necessary for Québec French to align itself on SF in order to rectify the abnormal linguistic situation referred to above. Probably the most important initiative in this sense was taken by the Québec state itself, in the early days of the Révolution Tranquille, through the specially created *Office de la Langue Française* which was made responsible for promoting correct usage. The OLF notably set in train an extensive and long-running project to create correct French terminologies in all the sectors of modern manufacturing and commerce where Québec French had adopted English or English-derived expressions. This exercise of linguistic recuperation can rightly be seen as socially and politically progressive in the historical circumstances of the time. Interestingly, the OLF's first director

---

standard et aménagement, Québec, Institut québécois de recherches sur la culture, 1996, p. 73).

Jean-Claude Corbeil used the term "aména-gement" to characterize this policy :

> *En résumé, tous les travaux de l'Office sont orientés vers un même but : permettre à la collectivité québécoise de prendre en main le destin de la langue française au Québec [...]. Par analogie, [...] nous utilisons pour la désigner l'expression "aménagement lin-guistique" comme on parle de l'aménage-ment du territoire*[6].

But the OLF also made pronouncements on the general language, alongside its work on the technical lexis, and here it could be said that its influence, at least initially, was less constructive. In 1967 it issued a list of expres-sions entitled *Les canadianismes de bon aloi* (1967) which does not seem entirely consis-tent with Corbeil's statement. By authorizing only a very few specifically North American

6. Jean-Claude CORBEIL, *Guide de travail en terminologie*, Québec, Ministère de l'Éducation du Québec, coll. "Cahiers de l'Office de la langue française", n° 20, 1974.

expressions as fit for use by speakers of good French, this document fostered the notion that, with very few exceptions, Québec French was not legitimate. Rather than "taking in hand" its own usage, Québec, by implication, had to follow standards laid down across the Atlantic. While the OLF itself passed beyond this initial phase, evolving in later years towards more a liberal stance, other commentators in the conservative camp have clung steadfastly to a more purist position. Such has been the case with the numerous guides to good usage[7] whose principal aim is to provide their readers with the approved SF terms to replace what are deemed incorrect or inappropriate local usages. At its most extreme, this purist position asserts that if Québec

---

7. Gérard DAGENAIS, *Dictionnaire des difficultés de la langue française au Canada*, Montréal, Éditions Pedagogia, 1967 ; Gilles COLPRON, *Les anglicismes au Québec*, Paris, Beauchesne, 1971 ; Marie-Éva DE VILLERS [ed.], *Multi-dictionnaire des difficultés de la langue française*, Montréal, Québec/Amérique, 1988.

adopted its own variety of French, it would be locked into a linguistic ghetto and unable to communicate with other French speakers throughout the world[8].

The *aménagiste* case, on the contrary, is that the standards which define good usage can only be determined within the linguistic community concerned. They share with Corbeil and OLF the sociolinguistic view of language which sees it as being strongly conditioned by its geographical and social environment. The more distinctive the language environment, the greater will be the variation in language usage and the greater the need for different language norms. After nearly four centuries of separate development, in a community far removed from its original source in Europe, Québec French has inevitably, in this view, taken on distinctive

8. See, for example, Lysiane GAGNON, "Oui, mais quelle langue ?", *La Presse*, April 1st 1989 and Annette PAQUOT, "Conception identitaire de la langue et enseignement du français", *La Presse*, March 14th 2001.

features of its own. To accept only the forms of the language known in France, must lead, as the purist position shows, to an attitude that stigmatizes French Canadian forms that are completely natural to a North American user of the language. The aim of the *aménagistes,* therefore, is to "repatriate" linguistic judgments[9] and elaborate a Standard Québécois along the lines defined by the Association Québécoise des Professeurs de Français in 1977 :

> *Le français standard d'ici est la variété du français socialement valorisée que la majorité des Québécois francophones tendent à utiliser dans les situations de communication formelle*[10].

---

9. Jean-Denis GENDRON, "Existe-t-il un usage prédominant à l'heure actuelle au Québec ?", Lionel BOISVERT, Claude POIRIER and Claude VERREAULT [eds.], *La lexicographie québécoise : bilan et perspectives*, Québec, Presses de l'Université Laval, 1989, p. 89.

10. Pierre MARTEL and Hélène CAJOLET-LAGANIÈRE, *op. cit.*, p. 77. The abbreviation SQ will be used in this sense. In

We are thus faced with a considerable conflict of attitudes and beliefs. At one level, there is a polemic among the intellectual élite arising from competing philosophies of language and ideologies, which explains why the exchanges are often heated. (There is not, however, an immediate equation between conservative and radical positions on language, on one hand, and politics, on the other. Some language conservatives are political nationalists and vice versa). At another level, and more innocently, there is a wider misunderstanding based simply on the fact that the issues have not been well documented until relatively recently. The notion that there is a Standard Québécois is recent and not yet in general circulation. Most Québécois, whether

---

addition QF (Québec French) will refer to the wider totality of Québec French including the vernacular. It should be noted that there are differences between QF and other varieties of North American French, especially Acadian. The issues discussed in this article relate to QF, but not necessarily to the other varieties.

highly educated or not, are in the position of M. Jourdain : they use SQ every day without explicitly realizing it. The signs of confusion are to be found in every user poll. When asked, the general public prefers many aspects of the Québec French that they actually use, but sees Standard French as more "correct" and therefore "superior"[11]. The same reactions can be found in every minority language community, and simply reflect the predominance of a prestigious norm and general uncertainty about the status of language varieties and how they are to be distinguished.

THE NATURE OF QUÉBEC FRENCH

It is no part of the *aménagiste* case to exaggerate the differences between language varieties. Quite on the contrary, it is freely admitted

---

11. Hélène CAJOLET-LAGANIÈRE, "Attentes et besoins du public québécois en matière de langue", Louis MERCIER and Claude VERREAULT [eds.], *Les marques lexicographiques en contexte québécois*, Québec, OLF/Gouvernement du Québec, 1998, p. 68.

that SQ is very close to SF, and in many respects becoming closer[12]. As a result of the normal processes of education and international exchange, many of the older vernacular expressions are disappearing in favor of standard counterparts. The large numbers of Québec people who follow events in France and watch TV5 will frequently adopt the words and expressions by which media events are transmitted to them, in the same way that citizens of the UK adopt expressions from the US and other parts of the English-speaking world. In this respect, language communities are no longer confined within national frontiers, and are increasingly permeable to influences from related cultures elsewhere and, in such a situation, Québec is much more likely to be influenced by France than vice-versa. Nevertheless, despite increasing conver-

---

12. Claude POIRIER, "Le lexique québécois : son évolution, ses composantes", René BOUCHARD [ed.], *Culture populaire et littératures au Québec,* Stanford, Anima Libri, 1980, p. 52.

gence, many distinctive usages continue to exist and thrive – there seems to be no law by which one can predict the survival or death of vernacular expressions. More particularly, despite increasing uniformization, the ambient language environment remains distinctive. As Britain and America are, in Bernard Shaw's famous aphorism, divided by the same language, so are Québec and France, and for the same socio-linguistic reasons.

If differences in language environments are not always fully understood, one reason is that their effect varies, depending on whether receptive or productive competence in the language is involved. In the receptive dimension, a language user can understand virtually every statement in that language, wherever in the world it may be coined[13]. If there are differences among varieties, these either pose no

13. Alain REY, "À la recherche de la norme : un dictionnaire québécois", Pierre MARTEL and Jacques MAURAIS [eds.], *Langues et sociétés en contact*, Tübingen, Niemeyer, coll. "Canadiana Romanica", vol. 8, 1994, p. 312.

receptive problem or can be quickly learned with minimum inconvenience. On first going to Québec, a user of another variety of French discovers distinctive expressions like *babillard, brigardière, blé d'Inde, dépanneur, magasiner, sacres, échapper une assiette* or *barrer une porte*. While in Québec, he may well learn to integrate these expressions into his productive competence, motivated by courtesy and a desire to blend into the language environment. But he will always be aware of them as "foreign" elements which are not part of his own normal production. Back in his own language context, these are not the expressions he would spontaneously use, except as conscious "quotations" from another language source. This is the phenomenon which, multiplied over hundreds of instances covering a wide spectrum of variation, adds up to the elusive but undeniable difference immortalised by Bernard Shaw.

PRONUNCIATION AND LEXIS

The two most obvious aspects of language in which variation occurs are pronunciation and lexis. Uniquely, the former arouses little controversy, because in SQ it is a feature that is so all-pervasive as to be unquestioningly accepted. Although some older pronunciations have disappeared from normal speech (the former [we] vowel sound, as in *moi, roi,* for example) other highly distinctive and equally old features (such as the affrication of *d/t* in certain positions) have been accommodated into the accepted norm[14]. To this extent, a norm for the spoken language in Québec is largely agreed upon, clearly different from the norm in France, with no serious disagreement between conservatives and *aménagistes*. But the existence of this variation has an obvious consequence if dictionaries produced in

---

14. Luc OSTIGNY and Claude TOUSIGNANT, "Introduction", *Le français québécois : normes et usages*, Montréal, Guérin, 1993.

France are used in Québec without adaptation to pronunciation guides.

Lexis remains the main area of dispute because it is the most accessible feature of language and the one that is most usually taken to define it. Since, as pointed out above, SQ shares the overwhelming majority of its words with SF, it is lexis that also gives rise to the claim that the two varieties are, at least in written form, indistinguishable. Typically, Québec journalists or intellectuals have denied that a separate SQ exists by instancing their own texts, supposedly written in a language identical to SF, when in fact they are marked by numerous *québécismes*[15].

As always, the flashpoint occurs around highly marked colloquial items, stigmatized by one camp but more tolerated by the other. Fortunately, however, the *aménagistes* have been able to move the debate forward by

15. Claude POIRIER, "Le français et les québécismes", *La Presse*, May 25th 1989.

drawing our attention to less contentious areas of lexis which distinguish SQ. Thus even purists will accept that something like 20 % of the total lexis is made up of legitimate Québec words, most of them in active daily use[16]. Many are words and usages that have remained more active in a particular sense in Québec than in France (*s'écarter* for *se perdre*, *venir* for *devenir*, *marier* for *épouser*, *menterie* for *mensonge*, *dispendieux* for *coûteux*) or simply have a greater frequency of use (*haïr*). But in addition, within the basic vocabulary stock shared with SF, the connotations that everyday words acquire through having functioned in different environments can vary significantly. This would appear to be the case even with such simple words as *innocent*, *avenue*, *cuisinière*, *torrent*, *fleuve*, *bois*, *pin*, *jaser* and *bas*[17],

---

16. Marie-Éva DE VILLERS, "Les marques lexicographiques : des points de repère essentiels pour l'usage des mots", Louis MERCIER and Claude VERREAULT [eds.], *op. cit.*

17. See Jean-Claude CORBEIL, "Le régionalisme lexical : un cas privilégié de variation linguistique" and Claude POIRIER,

and it is not an exaggeration to say that examples of this phenomenon are endless. A word such as *province* cannot be used in Québec in many of the uses it has in France (*une petite ville de province, vivre en province, un jeune provincial frais débarqué,* etc. can all be recognized but not produced). Every Québécois knows the verbs *casser* and *aboyer* but the verbs most frequently used are *briser* and *japper. Congère,* if it is known, will never be used : *banc de neige* is the only acceptable term. *La colonisation* is a well known historical term in each country but what it refers to is radically different in each case. *Un petit suisse* is not the same thing in Québec as in France. The effects of connotation, frequency of use and historically determined differences of reference, are so widespread that these aspects

---

"Les avenues de la lexicographie québécoise", both in *La lexicographie québécoise : bilan et perspective,* and Jean-Claude BOULANGER, "Le pacte normatif du français québécois : réflexions sur les marques lexicographiques diatoniques", Louis MERCIER and Claude VERREAULT [eds.], *op. cit.*

of language alone would justify the existence of separate dictionaries, as we shall see.

In addition SQ, as an autonomous variety, has proved fertile in adding to the lexical stock of French. If, in one respect, modernization has moved SQ nearer to SF, in other respects it has also fostered distinctiveness, because an expanding modern society naturally creates new cultural practices and new institutions of its own, which trigger new indigenous vocabulary. At the level of morphology, the feminization of titles occurred in Québec long before France, and is still more extensive and less contentious – a small but culturally revealing distinction. There are extensive areas of terminology, from geography (*nordicité*), culture (*téléroman*) and education (*collège, cégep, polyvalente,* even *baccalauréat*), to health care (*virage ambulatoire*), social security and government (one of the most fertile areas of distinctive lexis), finance (*REER*), and telecommunications (*courriel*) where new coinages have multiplied. Often, new technical terms will take on extended meanings (*échéancier*), some of which have spread elsewhere in *la francophonie*[18].

But to limit discussion to discreet lexical items is to miss a key aspect of the subject. Rather than being simply a matter of individual words, it is as much in their combination and structuring into discourse that the distinctiveness of a variety occurs. Since every culture has its own traditions and habits of thought, it also generates its own patterns in language, and its own rhetorical strategies[19] which in turn lead to characteristic associations of words. These range from set idioms and expressions, of which there is a large number, many of them vernacular but many also used in SQ (*c'est de valeur*), to looser collocations of words habitually grouped together either semantically or syntactically.

---

18. Jean-Claude BOULANGER, *ibid.*, p. 181.
19. Alain REY calls them *stratégies de discours* ("Intervention in discussion", *La lexicographie québécoise : bilan et perspective*, p. 168).

Hence connotation and difference of meaning can occur in a grouping of words that in themselves are not distinctive. The expression *l'aménagement du français* itself carries an immediacy of meaning and implications for a Québec speaker that it does not have in SF, and the same would be true of, for example, *le fait anglais* and a host of others[20].

What this points to is the influence on meaning of paradigmatic clusters of words. It is because of the paradigm of constitutional terms in which it occurs in Québec that the word *province* cannot function in the same way as in France. Similarly it is because of paradigmatic relationships that the choice of terms to refer to a car is not the same in SQ as in SF[21]. One of the terms, *le char*, comes from

---

20. Pierre MARTEL, Nadine VINCENT and Hélène CAJOLET-LAGANIÈRE give many others examples in "Le français québécois et la légitimité de sa description", *Revue québécoise de linguistique*, vol. 26, n° 2, 1998, p. 97-106.

21. Claude POIRIER, "Le lexique québécois : son évolution, ses composantes", p. 55.

the historic vernacular and in everyday use has been replaced by SF terms, but it survives very possibly, like many other vernacular terms, because it allows for stylistic variation within the paradigm. In this case *le char* can carry a tone of affectionate irony not present in *voiture* or *auto*, similar to the tone that English speakers sometimes obtain by referring to their car in the feminine. Elsewhere, other historic vernacular terms will be used as a fleeting mark of national identity, even though the user will normally choose the corresponding SF terms for everday purposes. Such relationships among words involve few or no difficulties of communication between SF and SQ users, but they generate important nuances of meaning that add up to a distinctive form of the language.

ANGLICISMS

Historically, anglicisms have been central to the whole concern about North American

French, an importance encapsulated in the title of Jules-Paul Tardivel's famous nineteenth century tract : *L'anglicisme, voilà l'ennemi !* (1880). But, as a result of the general social progress of Québec, that situation has now changed dramatically. On the one hand, as linguistic normality has been restored, there has been a marked reduction in the number of borrowings in common use. On the other hand, there is now also a growing awareness, in every sector of opinion, that all world languages, including SF itself, are exposed to the invasive influence of English. France, despite its position as a powerful nation with a prestigious culture, has had to follow the example of Québec in enacting legislation to protect its language in its own public arena. As a result, there is no longer a tendency to hold up Québec as a unique case of French adulterated by English and anglicisms no longer dominate the language debate.

Nevertheless history has given anglicisms a distinctive place in North American French, and in some cases they still divide the linguistic camps. In France, anglicisms have been introduced through the intellectual and fashionable interests of the middle classes, and, more recently, via youth culture and pop music. As a result, they have mainly retained their original form as manifest borrowings. In Québec, on the other hand, they were more extensively adopted by the working class and have penetrated more deeply into both the sound system and morphology of the receiving language[22]. Hence, the more popular and familiar the register, and the longer they have been established in popular use, the greater the degree of transfiguration in form (*enfirouapé, bécosse, mâche-mallo, l'apenouillère*) or meaning (*une fille bien le fun, ma blonde, son chum, smatte*). But their double identity as anglicisms originating in the vernacular makes them typical of the language

22. *Ibid.*, and Claude POIRIER, "Problèmes et méthodes d'un dictionnaire général du français québécois", *Revue québécoise de linguistique théorique et appliquée*, vol. 7, nº 1, p. 13-45.

features deprecated by purists, who tend to associate popular usage with debased language and often prefer an outright anglicism if it is used in France to a correct French term used only in Québec : *square*, for example, is recommended in preference to *carré* as an architectural term[23]. The *aménagistes*, on the contrary, are more disposed to welcome naturalized anglicisms as a manifestation of linguistic creativity which enriches the language and gives QF a flavour of its own. This particular class of terms thus falls into the main territory of dispute about language variety and the extent to which they will become fully embedded as acceptable items in SQ will depend on the outcome of the current debate.

One also finds in SQ many expressions which give the impression of being anglicisms (*incidemment, présentement, habiletés*), although in fact they exist in SF, but are not used

---

23. Marie-Éva DE VILLERS [ed.], *Multi-dictionnaire des difficultés de la langue française.*

as extensively or in the same stylistic ways in that variety. Rather than being anglicisms in the strict sense, therefore, they illustrate the general tendency for words to acquire different frequencies and types of use as they cross the Atlantic, and in these cases they seem to do so under the influence of corresponding words in English. Many such "false anglicisms" occur in political and economic journalism, possibly reflecting the fact that the sources of documentation and published research used by Québec journalists will be very largely American. In this respect, although they do not clash fundamentally with the general French idiom of the writing in which they occur, they act as stylistic markers which point to the Québec language environment.

GRAMMAR

Space precludes a full discussion of grammar, but the reader should at least be aware that variation is also to be found in this aspect of language. It has elicited less public discussion so far, because the main activity of *aménagement* has been in lexis. Yet a comprehensive study of the grammar of QF exists[24] and an increasing number of detailed studies are appearing in academic journals. All of these sources give evidence of departures of various kinds from the grammar of SF. This is hardly surprising. If even a highly regulated language like SF experiences changes in grammar over time[25], one would expect grammar also to vary as a result of transfer to a different environment.

DICTIONARIES

The publication of dictionaries has been, with education, the main field to which *l'aménagement* has applied itself, and it is largely

24. Jean-Marcel LÉARD, *Grammaire québécoise d'aujourd'hui*, Montréal, Guérin, 1995.
25. Henriette WALTER, *Le français dans tous les sens*, Paris, Laffont, 1988.

through the controversy aroused by these dictionaries that the language debate has been brought to the attention of the general public. The focus on dictionaries is no more than one would expect. Where a language community has a strong sense of its distinctiveness, there is inevitably a demand for dictionaries to reflect its specific usages, but often a certain amount of opposition to such innovation. One celebrated example of this is Webster's dictionary of American English, which was the linguistic counterpart of the Declaration of Independence of the United States, but was not received with unanimous favor. Elsewhere in the English-speaking world, the same phenomenon can be seen, not least – in more recent times – in English-speaking Canada. New Canadian dictionaries of English make a positive virtue of their specific national nature. The Penguin dictionary proclaims its "100 % Canadian content", while the Oxford Dictionary of Canadian English, after noting in its preface that Canadian English was initially scorned as an uncouth dialect, asserts that English Canadians now take pride in their own variety.

The situation has been different in the French-speaking world, however, where the high diversity of usage throughout *la franco-phonie* has been in manifest contrast with the exclusive domination of dictionaries emanating from France, reflecting (until very recently) only SF usage. In this context, it is revealing that Québec has been the exception to the rule, even prior to the emergence of the *aménagiste* project. The ambition to record the distinctive form of French that has evolved in Canada goes back at least to the end of the nineteenth century with the formation of *la Société du Parler Français au Canada,* but found its first major expression in dictionary form in Bélisle's *Dictionnaire général de la langue française au Canada* in 1957. What distinguished this dictionary from previous glossaries or differential dictionaries (i.e., those that catalogue only distinct vernacular terms) was that the French-Canadian lexical items which it recorded were presented as integral parts of the French language in general. Nevertheless this pioneering effort was the result of a compromise since its method was simply to expand an already existing SF dictionary by augmenting it with French Canadian terms. This is a significantly different procedure from attempting a complete description of how *all* French words are used in North America.

A more ambivalent milestone was reached in 1980 when Léandre Bergeron published his *Dictionnaire de la langue québécoise,* with a preface entitled *La charte de la langue québécoise,* vigorously making the case for the distinctiveness of QF. While this dictionary is not without merits, Bergeron spoiled his case by vastly exaggerating the difference between Québécois and French, speaking in terms of separate languages rather than of distinct varieties[26]. As

---

26. Claude Poirier [ed.], *Dictionnaire du français plus,* Montréal, Centre éducatif et culturel, 1988, p. 135.

a result he tends to favor the supposedly colorful popular registers, where QF is at its most distinctive, over more formal registers, thereby blurring the distinction between a dictionary and a glossary of the vernacular language[27]. The outcome was inevitably a hostile reaction from those who feared that the notion of a distinct variety could only lead to greater vulgarity in the language.

Since Bergeron, however, Québec lexicography has made great strides. On the basis of a large volume of theoretical and applied research, there has been an increasing flood of lexicographical publications of different kinds. Among these, three dictionaries are particularly significant and represent the main

---

27. Lionel MENEY (*Dictionnaire québécois français*, Montréal, Guérin, 1999). This work, although excellent on its own terms, falls into the same trap by encouraging the notion that SF speakers need a "bilingual" dictionary to understand QF. He can only sustain this fiction by giving pride of place to vernacular registers rather than the standard language. The work is thus the best current glossary of popular expressions, rather than a dictionary in the full sense of the word.

achievements of the *aménagiste* project to date. The *Dictionnaire du français plus* (1988) and the *Dictionnaire historique du français québécois* (1998) are both edited by Claude Poirier, who leads the long-running research project known as *Le Trésor de la langue française au Québec*, based at Laval University. The *Dictionnaire québécois d'aujourd'hui* (1992, new edition 1993) is edited by Jean-Claude Boulanger, also based at Laval.

The DFP and DQA are general dictionaries of French, aimed at the general public, and based on the premise of SQ being a distinctive variety. Like Bélisle they both derive from dictionaries already published in France (by Hachette in the case of *DFP* and by Le Robert in that of *DQA*). The crucial distinction from Bélisle, however, is that the source works have been entirely revised and adapted for North American use. As well as having a vastly greater range of specific North American vocabulary, the entries concerning the common core of French vocabulary define words as they are used in North America, rather than in Europe. In the great majority of cases, there is no marked difference from the treatment accorded to the same words in the source works. In other cases, however, the treatment is different in a variety of ways. North American examples are naturally used rather than European ones (*le bas Saint-Laurent* rather than *le bas Rhin*)[28] and, especially, there is a full recording of all the *nuances* of meaning, connotation, frequency of use and extended use (addition of *le Bas du Fleuve* to the above example) which give a different profile to many words for a Québécois user. Perhaps controversially, as we shall see, they extend the logic of this approach by reversing the convention hitherto applied to descriptive labeling of items. Distinctive labels for Québec words or usages are not used, since the readership is assumed to take Québec usage

28. Each also has an encyclopedic section in which Québec geographical, historical and social data have been incorporated into the original entries compiled in France.

for granted. Instead differences of use in other francophone countries, including France itself, are signaled by descriptions such as *surtout en France, en France* and *francisme* to draw attention to a different meaning or association for a Québec user. The latter include not simply words which relate to French institutions that do not exist in North America (*préfet*), but also common words that are virtually never used in Québec, but are part of the "passive" general vocabulary of any French speaker (*marron, enquiquiner*).

The *DHFQ* differs from the other two in being a differential, rather than a general, dictionary, but it gives much more extensive historical information on the derivation and evolution of lexical items than previous differential dictionaries. Its second original feature is to apply this treatment not only to specifically French Canadian words, but also to words belonging to the core vocabulary of French (even such simple words as *pain* and *bois*, among others) which have evolved differently in Québec. In this respect, the *DHFQ* represents the blueprint of the lexicographic philosophy which has been applied in the two general dictionaries. In due course, it will presumably become a multi-volume work which will underpin the general dictionaries with a fuller, more scholarly treatment of large parts of their corpus. For the moment, it is a work in progress which draws on only a fraction of the documentation which the Laval research team has compiled in more than 20 years of research, but it is one that shows the high level of scholarship that is now devoted to the subject.

Taken together, these three publications can be said to have established the scholarly case for the recognition of a distinctive SQ. The validity of the case is now well accepted internationally, not least in France itself. It is somewhat ironic, that while some in Québec continue vociferously to insist on rigorous adherence to the norms laid down in France[29],

29. Diane LAMONDE, *Le maquignon et son joual. L'aménagement du français québécois*, Montréal, Liber, 1998.

informed French opinion is moving in the opposite direction. Dictionaries published in France now regularly include entries concerning usage in other francophone countries, especially in Québec[30], and there is increasingly close collaboration between French lexicographers and their Québec colleagues. The publishing house of *Le Robert*, headed by Alain Rey, is the most closely involved : a team from *Le Robert* worked collaboratively with Jean-Claude Boulanger on the *DQA*, making it the product of a unique transatlantic partnership.

Yet in Québec itself, while all three works were warmly welcomed by knowledgeable

---

30. Another sign of this widening interest was the publication in 1997 by Hachette of the first *Dictionnaire universel francophone (www.francophonie.hachette-livre.fr)*, the stated aim of which is to give equality of status to all the varieties of French within *la francophonie*. No less significant is a renewed interest in regional varieties within France : see, for example, Pierre RÉZEAU [ed.], *Dictionnaire des régionalismes de France. Géographie et histoire d'un patrimoine linguistique*, Bruxelles, Duculot, 2001.

commentators, the general press reception was largely hostile, to the extent of affecting the commercial success of the two general dictionaries. The hostility from conservative quarters was predictable, simply on grounds of principle, which is why it affected even the *DHFQ*, a model of enlightened scholarship it would be hard to fault. But it was especially the *DQA*, in its first edition (1992), which fuelled the worst fears of the *anti-aménagistes* by somewhat misjudging the extent to which it could include vulgar colloquialisms. Even some admirers of the volume conceded that editorial policy had been over-permissive in this respect, given the sensitivity of public opinion on language issues in Québec. As a result a revised edition (1993) was hurriedly issued, in which the offending items were either withdrawn or were more clearly marked as being vulgar in register. While this remedial action has adequately corrected what was never more than a marginal flaw, affecting a mere handful of items, the more fundamental damage was that done to the concept of SQ itself. Opponents felt reinforced in their belief that recognizing Québec usage essentially meant trying to legitimize vulgarisms and lowering language standards and with rare exceptions ignored the positive achievements of both *DQA* and *DFP*[31].

A second bone of contention was the decision in both *DFP* and *DQA* to take Québec usage, including the common core of French vocabulary, as the norm, and label only departures from Québec usage. Lexicographers here tend to divide according to their wider convictions, rather than on simply professional grounds. Conservative linguists allege that Québec readers will feel more linguistically secure by knowing how their usage diverges

31. A good example of a review facing both ways is that of Philippe BARBAUD ("*Le dictionnaire québécois d'aujourd'hui* : coup de Jarnac", *Québec français*, n° 90, 1993), who virulently attacked DQA's supposed concessions to vulgarisms, while recognizing the great progress in description of SQ that it represented.

from that in France[32], while *aménagistes* believe that this perpetuates the ambiguity of a norm situated outside the language community. There is limited evidence that, if directly asked, poll respondents prefer the former position of having *québécismes* specifically labeled[33], but this may well be a conditioned belief. It is a well known feature of polls on language that reponses are often colored by insecure reactions from users of a minority variety[34].

32. But the terms in which de Villers states her belief are sometimes ambivalent. An example is her statement: "le locuteur [québécois] aura le choix entre des mots partagés par tous les francophones de la planète ou uniquement par ses compatriotes, voire par les seuls habitants de sa région" ("Les marques lexicographiques : des points de repère essentiels pour l'usage des mots", p. 160). This may give the impression that, throughout *la francophonie*, only *québécismes* fail to conform to general French usage. If so, this is the myth of *le français international* and is plainly false, as the *Dictionnaire universel francophone* quoted in note 29 testifies.

33. Hélène CAJOLET-LAGANIÈRE, "Attentes et besoins du public québécois en matière de langue", p. 69.

34. Marie-Louise MOREAU, "Pluralité des normes et des appartenances", *Terminogramme*, vol. 91-92, 1999, p. 49.

In practice, the issue seems often less acute than the positions adopted on principle imply. There seems little to choose between the way many SQ items are reported in the ostensibly conservative *Multidictionnaire* and in *DFP* or *DQA,* and compromises are clearly possible[35]. In large measure the most sensible practice will depend on the kind of readership that editors have in mind. For a public interested in full linguistic descriptions, including the etymology and history of words, national variants may be enlightening, but this will be less true of readers seeking the level of information that shorter dictionaries generally provide – and both DFP and DQA deliberately chose the short, general dictionary format as being the most useful one at the present juncture. What the majority of Québécois, who will spend their lives in their own language community, need to know is, for example, how to spell *vadrouille,* the only word for this

---

35. Claude CORBEIL, *Dictionnaire du français plus,* p. 42.

domestic implement that they know, rather than that the French *serpillière* (or, more remotely still, *wassingue*) in this sense. In any case, the growing number of specifically Québec items to be recorded will make labeling them all as *québécismes* appear increasingly inflationary and superfluous[36], especially in the context of a short dictionary.

Taking the long view, the commercial failure of *DFP* and *DQA* seems only a temporary phenomenon. What it tells us is that language is an area of human behaviour in which conservatism is deep-seated and in the case of Québec perhaps understandable. But their very existence, together with that of *DHFQ*, has radically changed the landscape and made the basic conservative assumption about language standards untenable.

The best proof of this can be found in the evolution that is taking place in the many

---

36. Jean-Claude BOULANGER, "Le pacte normatif du français québécois : réflexions sur les marges lexicographiques diatoniques", p. 181.

guides to good usage which have traditionally dictated standards in Québec. Where such works have tended in the past to indulge in outright condemnation of North American expressions, outside the restricted list of *canadianismes de bon aloi*, there is now a more open acceptance of legitimate Québec usage. While the second edition of Dulong's authoritative *Dictionnaire des canadianismes* (1999) continues to include the hitherto inevitable symbol signifying *à proscrire*, it is actually applied to very few terms, mainly now obsolete anglicisms, with the result that the contrast with Dulong's own pride in the linguistic richness of Canadian French is even more marked than in the first edition[37].

---

37. Gaston Dulong is a distinguished dialectologist. The fact that he ever felt obliged to combine such a scholarly interest with a proscriptive approach is as good an indication as any of the conformist linguistic pressures which were rife at a certain stage in Québec.

Even more significant are the change of title and editorial policy in what is usually considered to be the flagship of the proscriptive approach : the *Multi-dictionnaire des difficultés de la langue française*. The 1999 edition of this work adopted the shorter title of *Multi-dictionnaire de la langue française*, a change that seems intended as a step away from the corrective emphasis. More revealingly, while in the 1988 edition the standard adopted was "*la norme du français international telle qu'elle est décrite dans les grammaires et les grands dictionnaires*" (i.e. as emanating from France), the 1999 edition adopts a stance with quite different implications, accepting that : "[t]out dictionnaire s'élabore en fonction de la norme sociale admise par les membres de la communauté linguistique à laquelle il est destiné." A *norme du français québécois* is now therefore recognized, together with a range of usages that can be classified as SQ. The prohibitive emphasis has not disappeared, since there has been no general revision of entries, but the difference in attitude from an unreformed purist work like Dagenais[38] is already perceptible and will no doubt become more marked in future editions.

This evolution clearly owes much to the distinguished lexicographer and former director of the OLF, Jean-Claude Corbeil, who chaired the supervizing committee and signed the prefaces from which the above statements are taken. Here Corbeil again shows his firm belief in the legitimacy of different national varieties of French, and specifically in that of Québec. Although differing from the *aménagistes* on tactics and details (notably on the labeling of different varieties), he is at one with them on the necessity of a complete description of QF as a self-sufficient variety, which is what the dictionaries seek to provide[39].

---

38. Gérard DAGENAIS, *Dictionnaire des difficultés de la langue française au Canada*, Montréal, Éditions Pedagogia, 1967, with many subsequent reprintings.

39. Jean-Claude Corbeil's position is made paticularly clear in his call to abandon the concept of *le français régional*

With such increasing recognition of the case for *aménagement*, in France as in Québec itself, one may expect the dictionary project to be revived, drawing lessons from its temporary set-back. The main handicap that it has suffered from until now, apart from internal resistance, has been the technical one of the absence of a comprehensive database of Québec usage. It is easy for the general reader to forget, or fail to realize, that the production of authoritative dictionaries depends on the prior existence of a detailed corpus of lexical

and to describe Québec French "*exactement comme si nous étions la seule communauté linguistique de langue française qui existât*" ("Le régionalisme lexical : un cas privilégié de variation linguistique", p. 60). This chimes perfectly with the phrase of another senior lexicologist, Jean-Denis Gendron, advocating "*une conception autonomiste de soi-même comme communauté linguiste*" ("Existe-t-il un usage lexical prédominant à l'heure actuelle au Québec ?", p. 89) and later demanding "*le rapatriement du jugement sociolinguistique*" ("Les arguments pour ou contre un projet de dictionnaire décrivant les usages du français du Québec", *Actes du colloque sur l'aménagement de la langue au Québec*, Québec, Conseil de la langue française, 1990, p. 37-38).

items from which to compile the works. In the case of SF and standard English this corpus has been in existence for several centuries, so that ongoing lexicographical work of recording change and updating has a firm foundation on which to work. In the case of Québec, however, the whole preliminary constitution of the corpus is still in progress, with several teams involved on different projects.

In the fullness of time, however, it is already clear that a still more comprehensive account of QF and SQ will be available which will feed into revised or new dictionaries and other types of publication. There will only be gain and no loss in such an outcome. The existence of dictionaries that inform users lucidly on the language environment within which they themselves live will in no way endanger the access of Québec speakers to the full richness of the French language as it is used in France and elsewhere. The demographic and political weight of Québec will never be sufficient to give it the relative autonomy that the

United States enjoys as a language community – if indeed such autonomy is even possible in the contemporary world. But the participation of Québec speakers in the wider francophone language community can only be enriched by the fuller appreciation of language variation that the work of Québec linguists is now making available.

CONTEXT AND INTEGRATION :
THE ALLOPHONE COMMUNITIES
IN QUÉBEC

Ines Molinaro

Contemporary liberal theorists continue to wrestle with the moral and practical dilemmas induced by cultural pluralism. The debate between liberals and communitarians that began in the early 1980s has broadened subsequently into a wide-ranging attack and defense of liberal theory and liberal democratic practices[1]. And yet, contemporary

---

1. The debate between liberals and communitarians has given rise to an analysis of liberal theory, which grants the autonomous individual the enjoyment of rights. Ronald BEINER

theorizing on liberal democracy exhibits a "binary conceptual picture" rooted in and derivative of the liberal/communitarian and universalism/particularism framework[2]. While binary oppositions can be useful analytic and heuristic tools, they can also be an impediment to the understanding of multifarious reality. This difficulty is no less apparent in the

---

provides a brief overview of the debate in *What's the Matter with Liberalism,* Berkeley, University of California Press, 1992, pp. 15-38. The detractors of modes of liberal democratic government maintain in particular that practical reality infringes every day on the basic democratic parameters – equality, public debate and participation. For example, the current means of obtaining consent, which consists in aggregating individual choices (and forms the most important basis of the legitimate exercise of power in liberal democratic regimes), is sparking increasingly severe criticism. Democratic debate is lacking as a result of the procedures of political participation and the substance of such debate. This poses an even greater problem when citizens must debate the very nature of the political community, its identity and its fundamental principles.

2. This is expounded on by Mary G. Dietz in "Merely combating the phrases of this world : recent democratic theory", *Political Theory,* vol. 26, n° 1, February 1998, p. 114.

current normative and explanatory defense of civil political culture/identity with its emphasis on citizenship. Political theorizing on nationalism turns on an analytic dichotomy that counterposes civic nationalism and ethnic nationalism. This conceptual dichotomy can be a powerful tool for analyzing the boundaries of the nation/national identity as they are contested, defended and amended over time. However, it is useless if we fail to recognize that at any given time and to varying degrees, national identities embrace elements that are both civic and ethnic. Any vision of civic nationalism demands a definition of the essentials of citizenship. Two opposing discourses dominate contemporary models of citizenship : a liberal-pluralist theory and a neo-republican or communitarian theory[3]. These abstract binary oppositions

_____

3. Beiner distinguishes three theoretical perspectives : liberal, communitarian and republican. He associates the communitarian model with exclusivism and particularism wherein membership is defined by belonging to a particular

clarify alternatives and suggest limits within which liberal democracy can accommodate cultural diversity without seriously jeopardizing cohesion and allegiance.

Admittedly, these remarks oversimplify the nuances of a rich and multifaceted body of work. Nonetheless, there does appear to be broad acceptance that the associative grounds for pluralist liberal democracies and the principled limits of accommodating diversity are to be found in a civic political culture[4]. In

---

cultural or ethnic group. The republican model emphasizes civic bonds and is presented as an alternative or "third way" between the procedural/universal vision (liberal) and the substantive/particularistic vision (communitarian). However, for Beiner, this "third way" may be theoretically incoherent and practically impossible. R. BEINER, *Theorizing Citizenship*, Albany, State University of New York Press, 1995, pp. 12-15.

4. For example, see : Michael IGNATIEFF, *Blood and Belongings : Journeys into the New Nationalism,* Toronto, Penguin Books, 1994 ; Will KYMLICKA, *Multicultural Citizenship,* Oxford, Oxford University Press, 1995 ; Yael TAMIR, *Liberal Nationalism,* Princeton, Princeton University Press, 1993 ; Jeff SPINNER, *The Boundaries of Citizenship : Race, Ethnicity,*

embracing and celebrating cultural diversity as a source of enrichment, liberal political theorists have rediscovered and identified civic political culture or nationalism as a prerequisite for avoiding exclusion and fragmentation, the twin threats to stable and effective liberal democracy. Civic nationalism or culture reaffirms basic liberal principles or universally valid principles of justice. These abstract principles – individual rights, equality of opportunity, rule of law, respect for difference and tolerance, democratic government – must transcend all manner of differences and competing conceptions of the good if individuals are to be free to choose and perhaps revise their ways of life. A civic political culture holds out the possibility of eliciting allegiance without demanding

---

and Culture, Baltimore, Johns Hopkins University Press, 1994. This argument is advanced by Adrian FLAVELL, "A politics that is shared, bounded, and rooted ? Rediscovering civic political culture in Western Europe", *Theory and Society*, n° 27, 1998, pp. 209-236.

cultural uniformity. Moreover, the idiom of citizenship remains "untainted", devoid of reference to ethnicity, race or gender, blurring incommensurable identities, differences and dominant hegemonies. However, political principles cannot generate a sense of belonging, allegiance and community. Fulfilling the legal criteria and discharging the obligations of citizenship does not make a citizen "one of us".

I do not offer a reappraisal of the theoretical grounds of civic political culture. Instead, my subject is the integration policies devised by the Canadian and Québec states in response to the normative imperative to tolerate cultural diversity and the pragmatic imperative to affirm the boundaries of their respective political communities. There is a reasonable correspondence between these policies and current theoretical endorsements of a shared citizenship that would transcend ethnocultural differences without abandoning either basic liberal democratic principles or tolerance of cultural diversity. I argue that the context within which these policies have been devised and deployed defines the allegiance to which both states aspire. Distinctive political and historical legacies shape particular forms of exclusion in the Canadian and Québec context despite recourse to universalistic formulations of the grounds of inclusion.

I begin, by necessity, with the Canadian model of integration as it sets the parameters within which the Québec state can develop plausible strategies to integrate immigrants and their descendants. Both the Canadian and Québec state are committed to creating an inclusive bounded national community, i.e. a community that does not exclude anyone. Their aspirations in this respect, as we will see, are different, if not contradictory. Both states have political and pragmatic reasons for promoting their respective policies that may have little to do with sensitivity to the needs and interests of ethnocultural communities. On the other hand, ethnocultural communities have their own interests and needs that condition their strategies or responses to the demands made on them. The treatment of the Canadian model of integration is necessary but brief, as I am primarily interested in the ongoing project undertaken by the Québec state to create an inclusive civic culture that would command the allegiance of all inhabitants within its territorial boundaries. I consider this project by privileging the perspective of allophone communities in Québec. The viability of constructing a pluralist French-speaking civic culture is predicated on the inclusion of immigrants and their descendants as full members of the Québécois collectivity. And the viability of this project, I must emphasize, depends on the will and ability to rethink the parameters of the Québécois identity.

THE CANADIAN MODEL

Integration in every sense (linguistic, political, social and economic) is a process, structured by an array of state policies, mediated by the dominant public myths, historical legacies and social norms of the collectivity, and conditioned by the public and private practices that escape state regulation. In theory, integration is a bilateral process in which immigrants and citizens at birth consent to some changes and some adaptation. In practice, integrative mechanisms are not well known[5]. The term "integration" is now more frequently used than "assimilation" and

---

5. Morton Weinfeld and Lori Wilkinson emphasize that, in fact, immigrants are primarily the ones who must adapt. According to them, the integration of immigrants may be an illusion in that adults may never integrate fully and only their children and grandchildren will be able to do so. Morton WEINFELD and Lori A. WILKINSON, "Immigration, diversity, and minority communities" in Peter S. LI [ed.], *Race and Ethnic Relations in Canada,* Don Mills (Ontario), Oxford University Press, 1999, pp. 64, 67.

"acculturation", which have more negative connotations. The rejection of assimilation is given official sanction in the Canadian policy of multiculturalism within a bilingual framework. Bilingualism and multiculturalism are policies that enable the Canadian state to demarcate a pan-Canadian identity and effectively allocate or withhold status among competing groups. The Official Languages Act (1969) and the policy of multiculturalism (1971 ; 1988) contributed substantially to the symbolic and cultural transformations of Canada in the post-war years[6]. The policy of multiculturalism emerged within a political context marked by pressures to respond to the reconstruction of the French Canadian political identity, the inter-group dynamics unleashed by the Royal Commission on Bilingualism and Biculturalism, and more broadly

6. Raymond BRETON, "The production and allocation of symbolic resources : an analysis of the linguistic and ethnocultural fields in Canada", *Canadian Review of Sociology and Anthropology*, n° 21, pp. 123-144.

the politicization and revival of ethnicity that swept across many Western states.

If it is difficult to judge the initial degree and intensity of support for multiculturalism among ethnocultural groups, it is evident that the active intervention on the part of the federal government was significant[7]. Prime Minister Trudeau regarded the idea of biculturalism as a serious threat to the project of defusing and defeating the claims of Québec nationalists. As is well understood, the rejection of biculturalism not only denies the principle of two founding peoples, it also

---

7. Breton notes that among the ethnocultural groups submitting briefs to the B&B Commission not all were opposed to the terms of reference of the Commission and among the relatively small number of ethnic organizations that did not submit briefs, more than half were from Ukrainian organizations. The federal government provided financial assistance and the mechanisms that allowed ethnic organizational elites to air their views. Raymond BRETON, "Multiculturalism and Canadian Nation-Building" in Alan CAIRNS and Cynthia WILLIAMS [eds.], *The Politics of Gender, Ethnicity and Language in Canada*, Toronto, University of Toronto Press, 1986, pp. 45-48.

implies an equality of cultures that levels the status of the French Canadians to one ethnic group among many others. The Canadian model of integration endorses an instrumental linguistic dualism and emphatically resists privileging or endorsing an official culture by affirming equality among cultural groups. The conception of language as a "neutral" tool of communication rather than a vehicle of culture logically undermines arguments for special or additional measures to protect and promote the French language in Québec. In rejecting territorial bilingualism, the Canadian state denied the reality of linguistic practices existent in 1969 and in the intervening years, official bilingualism has not reversed substantially this fact[8].

_____

8. In 1996 86 % of the Canadian francophone population lived in Québec and 76 % of francophones living outside Québec lived in New Brunswick (accounting for 32.2 % of the New Brunswick population) and Ontario (accounting for 4.7 % of the Ontario population). The onus of bilingualism falls primarily on francophones outside Québec of whom

The disassociation of language and culture would appear to permit the Canadian state to claim to be "neutral" with respect to an individual's choice of official language or cultural identity. However, Will Kymlicka's interpretation of the Canadian policy is that a liberal state cannot be neutral when it comes to language and culture. In fact, he argues, the Canadian policy promotes and legally requires immigrants and their descendants to integrate into either the francophone or anglophone

---

84 % identify themselves as bilingual whereas only 7 % of anglophones outside Québec consider themselves bilingual. Across the country the rate of bilingualism among francophones (41 %) is almost five times higher than among anglophones (9 %). The territoriality of linguistic practices is further reflected in the fact that self-reported bilingualism among anglophone Quebecers (62 %) is almost twice that of francophone Quebecers (34 %). Among the 25 census metropolitan areas, the highest percentage of bilingual people is to be found in Montréal (49.7 %). STATISTICS CANADA, "1996 Census : mother tongue, home language and knowledge of language", *The Daily*, December 2nd 1997, p. 5.

societal culture[9]. This assessment is contradicted by the official state policy that has resolutely refused "to convert the dominant English-Canadian and French-Canadian cultures into an official pan-Canadian culture"[10]. Nonetheless, Kymlicka maintains that a policy of multiculturalism does not mitigate the need for integration into a societal culture ; such integration is "part of the 'nation-building' project in which all liberal

---

9. A societal culture is defined as "a territorially concentrated culture centered on a shared language that is used in a wide range of societal institutions, including schools, media, law, the economy, and government." Will KYMLICKA, *Finding Our Way. Rethinking Ethnocultural Relations in Canada*, Toronto, Oxford University Press, 1998, p. 27.

10. "The ideology of the state has distanced itself from the notion of two 'founding peoples' (or 'founding races') with its strongly ethnic overtones." The Supreme Court in the *Mahé* decision (1990) held that "[T]he general purpose of s.23 is clear : it is to preserve and promote the two official languages in Canada and their respective cultures…" Stacy CHURCHILL, *Official Languages in Canada : Changing the Language Landscape*, Ottawa, Department of Secretary of State Canada, coll. "New Canadian Perspectives Series", 1998, pp. 79-80.

democracies have engaged"[11]. This author considers that the conditions of liberal democracy require "thin" societal cultures, tolerant of diversity of religion, lifestyles, personal values and family relationships. The shared values or principles that constitute the minimal demands for inclusion, implicit in the Canadian multicultural policy, include respect for liberal-democratic norms, including individual rights and sexual equality (embodied in the *Charter of Rights*), respect for difference and tolerance towards others and the acquisition and use of one of the official languages of Canada. In essence, aside from the fact that Canada recognizes two official languages, the requirements for full inclusion are consistent with universally valid principles of justice associated with liberalism and a civic political culture. Practically speaking, the Canadian policy of bilingualism in a multicultural framework has had only partial success in

---

11. Will KYMLICKA, *op. cit.*, p. 28.

affirming an inclusive cohesive bounded national community. I will limit my remarks to a few aspects of the Canadian model that have a specific impact on the Québec project.

Official bilingualism has not been able to overcome the initial opposition of many Québécois francophones and Canadian francophobes. For them, multiculturalism and equality of individuals (guaranteed under sections 15 and 27 of the *Canadian Charter*) are incompatible with the objective of promoting the collective rights of language minorities. For Québécois francophones, the crux of the problem lies in Québec's sovereignty in terms of language and cultural policies. This claim is rooted in the conviction that the protection and promotion of French is more the responsibility of the Legislative Assembly of Québec than the Canadian judicial system or government. The language regime advocated by the Canadian state goes against this claim and its consequence: exclusive English Canada-Québec duality.

In addition, not only is official bilingualism rejected by francophone Québécois but the coherency and adequacy of multiculturalism is attacked by, among others, self-described Canadian nationalists as well as some members of ethnocultural groups whom the policy was intended to benefit. For ethnocultural groups, this policy marginalizes or ghettoizes ethnic or racial minorities, while Canadian nationalists disagree with what they consider to be privileges granted to ethnic minorities. There is also a fear that the policy encourages ethnic groups to preserve their own culture to the detriment of societal cohesion and the Canadian national identity[12].

---

12. The most recent national survey on Canadians' view of multiculturalism yielded contradictory findings. The majority of respondents (61 %) support the policy but the survey was unable to determine clearly whether they approve of the actual policy or the general ideals of equality and non-discrimination. The survey was conducted in 1991 by the Angus Reid Group and submitted to Multiculturalism and Citizenship Canada in a document titled *Multiculturalism and Canadians : National Attitude Survey, August 1991*. An

In his most recent treatment of Canadian multiculturalism, Kymlicka endorses the thrust of the policy in its current form, but advocates an explicit statement of the necessary limits of accommodating cultural diversity[13]. Once again, he pleads with Canadians to recognize that theirs is a multinational state and reiterates his thesis that liberal democracy has the capacity and obligation to accommodate the rights of self-government for minority nations. Kymlicka sustains the distinction between immigrants or ethnocultural groups and national minorities and defends the

---

analysis of the survey findings is provided in Peter S. LI, "The multicultural debate" and Raymond BRETON, "Intergroup competition in the symbolic construction of Canadian society" in LI [ed.], *op. cit.*, chap. 6 and 10.

13. The Economic Council of Canada recommended adjustments to the current multicultural policy, specifically endorsing the motion of a "moral contract" between immigrants and the host society that would make explicit the existence of official cultures in Canada. ECONOMIC COUNCIL OF CANADA, *New Faces in the Crowd*, Ottawa, Supply and Services Canada, 1991.

demands to integrate into the societal culture that can be made legitimately on the former but not the latter. By extension, the demands on immigrants and their descendants within the societal culture that is francophone Québec are no different than the demands made by the anglophone societal culture outside francophone Québec[14]. Kymlicka is clear on this point : he recognizes that pan-Canadian nationalism in the form of nation-wide bilingualism has allowed anglophones within Québec to perceive themselves as having a societal culture and an interest "in being able to ensure that newcomers to Québec from other provinces or other countries can integrate into their societal culture[15]." According to the reasoning of the federal integration policy, the existence of two societal cultures in Québec should enable immigrants to choose

---

14. Will KYMLICKA, *op. cit.*, pp. 28-29.

15. Will KYMLICKA, *op. cit.*, p. 157. See also recommendations of the *Task Force on English Education* (1992).

freely between them. Generally speaking, the rest of Canada does not offer immigrants this choice. In this respect, Québec sovereignists consider the Canadian policy a constraint that hinders the efforts made by the Québec state to encourage the establishment of the exclusive ties of loyalty to which it aspires[16]. This thinking must be taken further in order to determine how immigrants can integrate into francophone societal culture, regardless of whether the people of Québec opt for independence in the future. The Canadian policy provides a good example of the limitations of the theory that the State can prescribe a sense of belonging.

Secondly, both Wayne Norman and Will Kymlicka have argued compellingly that shared values or abstract principles in themselves are insufficient grounds in a multina-

---

16. For sovereignists, the solution is to establish a sovereign Québec. See Michel SARRA-BOURNET, "Comment devient-on québécois ?" in *Le pays de tous les Québécois. Diversité culturelle et souveraineté*, Montréal, VLB, 1998, p. 143.

tional state to secure solidarity and allegiance to an overarching political identity[17]. Collective myths, symbols, ethnicity, a shared history and memory are stronger sources of identity and have a greater purchase on allegiance than shared values. Nonetheless, shared values are precisely what Kymlicka identifies as sufficient grounds for forging a collective political identity or centripetal bond that would bind immigrants and their descendants to the dominant societal culture. On the one hand, the ability to reason through differences would require a degree of commonality or consensus. On the other hand, universal or abstract principles are combined in distinct ways with particularistic societal cultures whose self-images – the legacies and

---

17. Wayne NORMAN, "The ideology of shared values : a myopic vision of unity in the multi-nation state" in Joseph H. CARENS [ed.], *Is Québec Nationalism Just ? Perspectives from Anglophone Canada*, Montreal, McGill-Queen's University Press, 1995, chap. 6 and Will KYMLICKA, *op. cit.*, chap. 13, particularly pp. 171-173.

representations of their historical and cultural personalities – reinforce the hegemony of the dominant culture. This hegemony can limit significantly the impact that ethnocultural communities can have on dominant representations and discursive practices and by extension their acceptance and inclusion in the societal culture. Additionally, we need to take seriously what can and cannot be shared. Let us not deny the formidable barriers imposed by collective memories and the distances to be overcome for the outsider simply to access (let alone identify with) the world of the insider[18].

18. "How indeed can a social and symbolic link be forged between individuals detached from the traditions and memories of the franco-Québécois? [...] And how can people who have newly arrived connect with this history, since *a priori* they are concerned strictly with the present and not the past of the society in which they live?" Free translation of Jocelyn LÉTOURNEAU and Jacinthe RUELLE, "Nous autres les Québécois", in K. FALL, D. SIMEONI and G. VIGNAUX [eds.], *Mots et représentations. Enjeux dans les contacts interethniques et interculturels*, Ottawa, Presses de l'Université d'Ottawa, 1994, p. 302. This dilemma is particularly stark in the context of Québec but no less relevant in Canada or other liberal democracies.

Thus, even if the conditions of integration do not explicitly make reference to ethnicity, integration requires validation in everyday life and can never be reduced to mere individual choice. I will now examine the efforts recently made by the Québec state to define the dimensions of a common civic or public culture.

THE QUÉBEC MODEL

The model of integration promoted by the Québec state has undergone a number of substantial refinements since 1978. The one constant is that they have all been formulated within the framework of the primary social contract between the Québec state and the Québécois nation. The *Charter of the French Language* more than promulgates an official language, it constitutes a moral contract that binds the Québécois nation to the Québec state. By ascribing a moral responsibility upon the state to secure the continued existence of the nation, the nation constructs a standard of authority by which to measure the state and its actions. Thus, both legitimacy and allegiance are subject to the capacity of the Québec state to fulfill its moral obligations to the nation. In an early assessment of the consequences of the Charter of the French Language, S. Arnopoulos and D. Clift stated that "[T]he monolithic character of society, largely derived from its minority status in Canada, will have to become pluralistic in light of the majority status it is asserting within Québec[19]". Indeed, this is precisely what francophone Québécois intellectuals and the Québec state in its official policy statements have been advocating since early 1980s. The direction of state policy has been to expli-

---

19. S. Mc Leod Arnopoulos and D. Clift, *The English Fact in Québec*, Montréal, McGill-Queen's University Press, 1980, p. 191. They refer to Bill 101 as a "Trojan Horse". The assumption would appear to be that the culture of francophone Quebecers is so weak that it can only hope to survive if it is hermetically sealed from outside influences. It also presupposes an essentialist conception of both "traditional" and contemporary culture.

citly divest ethnic origin as a source of privilege or authority and to disassociate language and ethnicity in a conscious attempt to redefine the boundaries of Québec. Decision-makers would like the term "Québécois" to extend beyond its more specific and politicized meaning to refer to all people who live within Québec's borders, regardless of their ethnicity and political convictions. And yet, the gradual broadening of the meaning of Québécois to denote a civic identity has not overcome its elemental association with the French-Canadian nation in Québec. The construction of a civic Québécois identity is mired by the "simultaneous presence and absence" of ethnic identity[20].

---

20. "[...] ethnicity has come to signify an outdated, traditionalist image of French-Canadianness. That the very word 'ethnic' has been articulated against ethnicity, when the two operate in tandem — are not only some of the strategies that flip ubiquity into absence." Greg ELMER and Bram ABRAMSON, "Evacuating ethnicity in Québécois", Québec Studies, vol. 23, Spring 1997, pp. 13-28.

The model of integration currently promoted takes the form of a moral contract between immigrants or ethnocultural communities and Québec society defined as francophone, democratic and pluralist[21]. Immigrants are asked to commit themselves to democracy, individual rights and liberties (including sexual equality), tolerance of cultural diversity and the French language as the common and official public language. In return the state commits itself to promoting tolerance and accommodating cultural diversity throughout intercultural policy. The Québec state defines its integration objective as midway between a policy of assimilation and a policy of multiculturalism. The intercultural policy has two broad goals : the integration of allophones into mainstream Québec society and the promotion of openness within Québec society towards members of cultural

21. See *Énoncé de politique en matière d'immigration et d'intégration*, Québec, Ministère des Communautés culturelles et de l'Immigration, 1990.

communities[22]. In effect, the intercultural policy and the Canadian policy of multiculturalism are substantially similar and recent calls to firmly define the limits of diversity (i.e., what is non-negotiable) by clarifying the commitments immigrants must make to Canada would further reinforce the correspondence between them. To the extent that the moral contract makes explicit the limits within which cultural diversity is to be accommodated and defines the duties of citizens to actively participate in the political life of the community, it diverges from the Canadian multicultural policy[23]. The Québécois state

22. For example, these goals are to be achieved by promoting equality of opportunity, a command of the French language and through education for democratic citizenship in a pluralistic society. See the policy proposal entitled *A School for the Future : Educational Integration and Intercultural Education*, Québec, Ministère de l'Éducation, 1997 and *Un Québec pour tous ses citoyens. Les défis actuels d'une démocratie pluraliste*, Conseil des relations interculturelles, 1997.

23. The Québec policy includes approximately 309 measures and engages 43 ministries and agencies. Coordination

has constructed the boundaries of the political community through the policies of official unilingualism, interculturalism and the *Québec Charter of Human Rights and Freedoms*. While the Canadian policy of multiculturalism denies a special status to the French Canadians, the Québec state officially and legally distinguishes between ethnocultural groups, anglophone Quebecers and aboriginal nations. The latter two are recognized as having unique historical rights and claims. Québec has formally recognized eleven First Nations within its territory with rights to self-

---

and harmonization are difficult, a challenge that is shared with its Canadian counterpart. The frontline ministries responsible for ensuring the acquisition and promotion of the use of the French language among immigrants and the socio-economic integration of immigrants and members of ethnocultural communities are the Ministère de l'Éducation and the Ministère des Relations avec les citoyens et de l'Immigration. The latter is given responsibility for developing harmonious intercommunal relations. *Bilan du plan d'action gouvernemental en matière d'immigration et d'intégration (1991-1994)*, Québec, Ministère des Affaires internationales, de l'Immigration et des Communautés culturelles, October 1995.

determination and granted exemptions from the requirements of Bill 101 to the Inuit, Cree and Naskapi nations. The anglophone community, recognized as an historic minority, has acquired legal guarantees to social and medical services in English and anglophones are exempt from the language of education provisions of Bill 101 (granted in 1984 under the so-called "Canada" clause)[24]. Moreover, laws and regulations must be drafted in English and French to have the force of law and English can be used in both the National Assembly and in court proceedings. The hierarchy that differential rights, privileges and immunities establishes is an admission that not all citizens are expected to relate to the collectivity in the same way.

24. Access to English language schools is made available to a child of a Canadian citizen who received most of his/her elementary or secondary instruction in Canada or a child who is a temporary resident. Community organizations, certified private establishments and ambulance services also are available in English.

The extensive data collected by the state to gauge whether the *Charter of the French Language* is having the desired effect attests to the priority the state attaches to linguistic practices. On the side of intercultural relations, the data and research is far less extensive. Nonetheless, the policy statements and plan of action developed and refined over the last decade (the most recent plan of action, "Zero exclusion", put forth by the Ministère de l'Éducation (MEQ) and the Ministère des Relations avec les citoyens et de l'Immigration (MRCI), focuses directly on racial and ethnic discrimination) are genuine attempts to confront the difficulties of accommodation and the need to sensitize the public and those who work closely with immigrants and their children to the demands that pluralism makes on the dominant culture. The Québec state, as reflected in its policy statements and programs, has committed itself to nurturing a sense of belonging through a common citizenry based on shared liberal democratic principles and a shared commitment to French as the common public language. For all the laudable efforts to promote what is essentially a civic political culture and a robust citizenship, how plausible and effective is this project? One way to begin to fashion an answer to these questions is to attempt to assess the choices that the allophone communities appear to be making with regard to language use.

INTEGRATION STRATEGIES OF ALLOPHONE COMMUNITIES

Allophones now outnumber anglophones and the possibilities of securing French as the common public language very much depends, as it has throughout post-war era, on the linguistic choices of the allophone population. There are inherent difficulties with this line of inquiry that must make all assertions tentative. In the first instance, the designation "allophone", originally used in the Gendron

Report[25], refined and extended the range of social and political identities within Québec. The desire and will among francophone Quebecers to integrate immigrants in the late 1960s was pivotal to the assertion of the hegemony of the French language. The designation "allophone" provides immigrants and their descendants, hitherto unnamed, with a distinctive label, devoid of any content and referents other than the French and English opposition. Immigrants, with ties and by implication allegiance to the anglophone community, "polluted" the traditional English/French duality and created confusion as to who is a "vrai Anglais". The term "allophone" levels the differences among immigrants, disguising the heterogeneity of their languages and identities as well as their material conditions and interests. Reduced to a uniform condition, immigrants carry the

25. Commission d'enquête sur la situation de la langue française et les droits linguistiques au Québec, étude 3, Québec, Éditeur officiel du Québec, 1972, pp. 2-3.

potential to "become anything". Their ambiguity is further reflected in the fact that they are at once potential allies (in the fight to preserve the French language) and potential foes (by aligning themselves with the anglophones or worse still integrating to the anglophone community, they threaten the relations of power between the majority and minority). Moreover, the privileging of language as the determinant of political identity determines who can speak with authority within the collectivity. The referent "allophone" accentuates the linguistic incompetence of the immigrant, who must defer to those who speak well or speak appropriately. And indeed, it was the claim to speak on behalf of the "allophones", the presumption to appropriate or incorporate immigrants, that placed the allophones in the middle of a rivalry that precedes their arrival ; the "allophone" is invariably the third "person" in a relationship structured by the opposition between Québec and English Canada, between anglophones and francophones. The linguistic choices allophones appear to be making reinforce their liminality and locate them on the boundaries of the subjective community. Nonetheless, the social and political integration enjoyed by immigrants and their descendants varies widely as does their sense of alienation from and identification with the Québécois collectivity. For these reasons among others, we must resist collapsing the diversity and multiplicity that the referent "allophone" invites.

In its documentation the Québec state employs a variety of terms to name immigrants and their descendants, but the commitment to a common citizenry (as well as sensitivity to criticism) is reflected in the transformations of the Ministère de l'Immigration (1968) into the Ministère des Communautés culturelles et de l'Immigration (1981), subsequently replaced by the Ministère des Relations avec les citoyens et de l'Immigration (1996). The deputy minister of the MRCI noted that the change in the name of the ministry reflected a recognition that the term "communautés culturelles" was perceived as a term of exclusion, too closely associated to ethnic origins and culture ; moreover, it implied a denial that culture is dynamic and that the process of migration has multiple influences on cultural identity[26]. The sensibility comes closer to capturing the fluidity and hybridity of identities detectable among the younger generation of allophones.

Measures of language integration are blunt instruments that provide rough indications of trends. Linguistic integration is a complex process but in the context of Québec it is even more so. If, as Kymlicka notes, immigrants readily accept to "integrate into an existing societal culture" and can appreciate that "their life-chances are tied up with

26. Ernst JOUTHE, Assistant Deputy Minister, Relations civiques, Ministère des Relations avec les citoyens et de l'Immigration, *Allocution prononcée lors du Colloque organisé par l'APEIQ sur le thème "De l'interculturel à la citoyenneté. Un plus pour la cohésion sociale ?"*, Montréal, May 9th 1997, pp. 3-5.

participation in the range of social institutions, based on a common language, which define that societal culture"[27], the situation for immigrants and their descendants is not as straightforward as it would appear to be in the rest of Canada. Linguistic choices are not simply or even primarily a reflection of ill will towards francophone Quebecers. It is widely agreed that one of the effects of Bill 101 has been to make command of the French language increasingly a criteria for employment, and thus a powerful material incentive to acquire proficiency in French. It remains the case, as it probably always will, that the English language is the dominant language of North America. Thus, immigrants and their descendants as well as francophone Quebecers are presented with a powerful incentive to acquire competency in English[28]. The data for

27. KYMLICKA, *op. cit.*, p. 28.
28. A recent study of earnings differentials among linguistic groups over the past three decades indicates that in 1990 bilingualism for anglophones and francophones (male and

1971-1991 reveals that the steady increase in the percentage of allophones with a knowledge of French has not diminished the percentage of allophones with a knowledge of English over the same period[29]. The most

female, full- and part-time) is highly rewarded in Québec. By 1990, unilingual anglophone males earned less than either bilingual or unilingual francophones or bilingual anglophones. For allophone males knowledge of English alone is more valuable than knowledge of only French, but bilingualism is even more valuable. Daniel M. SHAPIRO and Morton STELCNER, "Language and earnings in Québec: trends over twenty years, 1970-1990", *Canadian Public Policy*, vol. 23, n° 2, 1997, pp. 116-140.

29. The data for allophones in the Montréal region is as follows:

	1971	1981	1986	1991
Knowledge of French:	47 %	62 %	66 %	69 %
Knowledge of English:	69 %	71 %	70 %	68 %
Knowledge of French and English:	33.1 %	44.6 %	47.4 %	46.6 %
Knowledge of French only:	14 %	17.7 %	18.9 %	22 %
Knowledge of English only:	35.8 %	26.1 %	22.3 %	20.9 %
Neither French nor English:	17 %	11.6 %	11.3 %	10.4 %

Data drawn from Comité interministériel sur la situation de la langue française, 1996, p. 274, published by the Office de la langue française, Données démolinguistiques, OLF web site.

recent data indicates that the percentage of allophones in the Montreal region with a self-assessed knowledge of French is slightly ahead of those who claim to have a knowledge of English. With respect to educational choices, the impact of Bill 101 is steadily apparent : in 1971, 90 % of allophone children were enrolled in English language schools ; by 1994-1995, 79 % were enrolled in French language schools. Perhaps more revealing is the percentage of allophones with the right to enroll their children in English language schools who choose to send their children to French language schools. The most recent figure of 8.7 % (1990) marks a substantial increase from only 3 % in 1983. Among anglophones there has also been an increase from 8.3 % in 1983 to 9.9 % in 1990. In addition, approximately one-third of all children in English language schools participate in French immersion programs[30]. While not negligible,

30. Data cited is for the Greater Montréal area that includes Montérégie, Montréal, Laval, Lanaudière, and les

the data does not allow us to conclude that without the restrictions of Bill 101, allophone parents would willingly choose to enroll their children in French language schools.

Demographers regard language transfers or mobility (rate established by comparing reported mother tongue and language used at home) as a useful indicator to measure linguistic assimilation. There is an inexorable intergenerational shift in language use and although the rate of loss varies for different ethnic groups, research suggests that within

---

Laurentides. Ministère de l'Éducation, Direction des études économiques et démographiques, fichier élèves-standard, cited by the Office de la langue française, "Langue et Éducation", OLF web site. It should be noted that allophones enrolled in English-language schools are mostly 2nd and 3rd generation Quebecers born in Québec who identify a language other than French and English as their mother tongue. The recent introduction of linguistic school boards may improve the rate of allophone students who continue their post secondary studies in French. Allophones who attended French language schools in the Protestant sector were less likely to continue their studies in French than those who attended French schools in the Catholic sector.

three generations knowledge and use of the heritage language declines dramatically. The 1996 Census indicates that over the past 25 years, the net shifts to French have increased more than those to English[31]. Among allophones, the proportion shifting to French was 39 % compared to 29 % in 1971. Overall there has been a decline in language shifts among allophones from 44 % in 1991 to 40 % in 1996. This is thought to be explained by the higher level of immigration during this period[32]. A

---

31. STATISTICS CANADA, *op. cit*. A further word of caution : data on language shifts or transfer is a measure of the percentage of people with a given mother tongue who speak another language most often in the home. The home language data reflects only the language most often spoken, and does not pick up instances where two or more languages are spoken at home (often the case in mixed families or if grandparents reside with the family). Moreover, home language does not in itself tell us if French is used outside the home on a daily basis, i.e. at work, in school, with friends, etc. The use of a language outside the home, particularly at school, serves as an important counterweight to the home language environment.

32. Of all immigrants living in Québec, 14 % immigrated between 1986 and 1990, while 23 % immigrated between 1991

more interesting phenomenon that speaks to the particular context of Québec is the higher rate of transmission of heritage language in Québec rather than in other regions. But here too we need to be cautious, as with all the statistics cited. Individuals reporting ability to speak a language do so on the basis of their own assessment. How should the phenomena of "ethnolects" or what sociolinguists refer to as "interlanguages" be interpreted ? Does the substantial borrowing and transformation of English and French words into the spoken heritage language indicate ethnic language retention or is it part of the process of assimilation[33] ? Another consideration may be that the bilingualism and trilingualism of allophones

---

and 1996. Forty-four percent of the foreign-born population immigrated before 1976. RECENSEMENT 1996, *Données ethno-culturelles*, "Populations immigrées recensées au Québec et dans les régions en 1996 : Caractéristiques générales", August 1998, p. 11.

33. Marcel DANESI, "Ethnic language and acculturation : The case of Italian-Canadians", *Canadian Ethnic Studies*, vol. 17, n° 1, 1985, pp. 48-103.

takes the form of diaglossa, where languages are used in different circumstances and are associated with different social roles[34]. Jean Laponce explains that diaglossic bilingualism (or trilingualism) can be relatively stable when the individual chooses to use a different language in the private domain (perhaps as a way of affirming one's ethnic identity), and in the public domain as an instrument of communication to participate in the wider community. In context of Québec, linguistic practices in the public domain have long been competitive and only relatively recently has the French-speaking majority succeeded in shifting the burden of bilingualism onto English speakers. The linguistic duality and the gradual equalization of the attraction of the two languages is widely held to be a

---

34. Jean A. LAPONCE, "Reducing the tensions resulting from language contacts : personal or territorial solutions ?" in Daniel BONIN [ed.], *Vers la réconciliation ? La question linguistique au Canada dans les années 1990*, Kingston, Institut des relations intergouvernementales, 1992, p. 125.

significant contributing factor in the retention of mother tongue and ethnic identity among allophones. However, it should not be assumed that there is a simple or straightforward connection between language and ethnic identity. In a small study of language and ethnic identity among a group of second-generation Quebecers of Italian origin, Anne-Marie Fortier reports that her respondents did not regard the ability to speak Italian as the defining trait of their identity, rather they cited particular practices, values, and cuisine as distinctively "Italian" traits. Of course, these traits reflect the particular social-historical world that Italian immigrants and their descendants have improvised within the context of Québec. Moreover, respondents cited their *multilingualism* in opposition to unilingualism and bilingualism, as a distinctive and positive trait of "allophone" identity[35].

35. Anne-Marie FORTIER, "Langue et identité chez des Québécois d'ascendance italienne", *Sociologie et société*, vol. 24, n° 2, 1992, pp. 91-102.

Language practices may be read as strategies that affirm the space between the hegemonies of French/English, anglophone/francophone, Québec/Canada. The apparent resistance to unilingualism need not be read as an obstacle to the generalization of French as the common public language of Québec.

It had been assumed that the children of immigrants, as the transitional generation, were caught between two irreconcilable worlds, saddled with multiple identity referents that invariably provoked a crisis of identity. Further, once the "transition" is effected, a uniform and unitary identity would emerge. However, recent research in both France and Québec suggests that children of immigrants express fluid ethnic identities and are comfortable with a plurality of ethnic identities[36]. The

---

36. D. Meintel notes that "[…] it is not strictly speaking a question of 'maintaining' but rather of continually transforming the characteristics that are still used as ethnic indicators […] We believe that the Montréal context has not only provided conditions conducive to perpetuating these ethnic

heterogeneity of cultural identity and the interrelationship of diverse cultures is a relatively new area of research in Québec. Such research may yield a more complicated but realistic account of the dynamic interpenetration of the multiple cultures. The diversification and hybridization of lifestyles evident in contemporary urban environments provide individuals with different and complex cultural options. We are still in the early stages of appreciating the instantiation of this phenomenon within the pluriethnic context of Montreal.

---

and cultural indicators, but has also offered the conditions of a very specific interethnic place [...] It should be noted that intercultural publications like *Vice-Versa*, *Parole métèque*, *Humanitas* and several others are found only in Montréal..." Free translation of D. MEINTEL, "L'identité ethnique chez de jeunes Montréalais d'origine immigrée", *Sociologie et société*, vol. 24, n° 2, Fall 1992, pp. 81-82, 85. See also D. MEINTEL, "Transnationalité et transethnicité chez des jeunes issus de milieux immigrés à Montréal", *Revue européenne des migrations internationales*, vol. 9, n° 3, 1993, pp. 63-79.

The inclination to assign a unifying and unitary identity to ethnic groups is not just convenient nor is it benign. The predisposition of the state to simplify and categorize is an essential means to enhance its administrative capacities and measure the effect of its policies. Nonetheless, these categories or standard designations are static and as such impose both an internal unity and an unqualified difference between cultural groups. The potential blurring of cultures and by extension the construction of identities that stress "both/and" rather than "either/or" is a palpable threat to an unqualified allegiance so valued by the modern nation-state[37].

---

37. Jocelyn Maclure emphasizes the need to recreate the Québécois identity between the comfort of an "authentic" Québec nation and the indifference of cosmopolitanism without roots. I agree with the author's defence of a profoundly pluralist Québécois identity that would accommodate the hybrid and fragmentary forms of cultural coexistence that prevail in contemporary Québec. J. MACLURE, "Authenticité québécoise. Le Québec et la fragmentation contemporaine de l'identité", *Globe. Revue internationale d'études québécoises*, vol. 1, n° 1, 1998, pp. 9-35.

FINAL THOUGHTS

The discourse of civic culture and citizenship has not depoliticized ethnicity nor effaced the relevance of the ethnic relations of powers within Québec (or Canada). The nation is not so easily transformed into a hegemonic culture. The integration strategies of so-called allophones are necessarily marked by resistance, driven by the impulse to overcome social subordination and the sense of political impotence[38]. The invisibility of

---

38. The Shapiro and Stelcner study provides evidence that language and ethnicity are related. Controlling for education, age and date of immigration does not change the results that regardless of education or time of arrival in Canada, or ability to speak English and/or French, allophones are still earning less than francophones and anglophones. Their estimates for 1990 indicate that French-speaking allophone men earned 23 % less than unilingual anglophones, 28 % less than unilingual francophones and 36 % less than bilingual francophones. These results do include controls for date of immigration. Earnings differentials among 40 "visible" and "non-visible" ethnic groups in Québec confirmed that several "non-visible" ethnic groups (Greeks, East Europeans and

ethnocultural minorities in educational institutions, the civil service, the media and spheres of public debate undermines the credibility of pretensions to overcome cultural monism. Yet, the full integration of immigrants and their descendants presupposes the will of the majority to open the *center*, to make space for the emergence and elaboration of a heterogeneous pluriethnic culture. Immigrants and their descendants born and raised in Québec are reminded everywhere and often that French is the common language of public discourse. The model of integration promoted by the Québec state seeks to elicit a deeper commitment than the use of the French language ; the larger goal is to develop among non-francophones a commitment to the preservation and empowerment of the French language. It may be that the French language

Latin Americans) incurred large and significant earnings penalties as did "visible" minorities (Arabs, Blacks, Chinese, South and West Asians and Native peoples). Daniel M. SHAPIRO and Morton STELCNER, *op. cit.,* pp. 121 and 130, note 22.

can only be a shared civic good, if it facilitates the elaboration of an open-ended, heterogeneous, multilingual civic identity.

THE EMERGENCE OF UNILINGUALISM :
ARCHEOLOGY OF THE LANGUAGE
ISSUE IN QUÉBEC

Karim Larose

Dispute about the "relationship between words and things" is said to be the "stuff" of politics[1]. The evolution of the language issue in Québec certainly provides striking evidence of this claim, marked as it is by long, hard debate over "words" used in reference to language, i.e. common terms and expressions that imply social and political stakes. Bitter controversy, for example, was fueled in the

---

1. Jacques RANCIÈRE, *Le partage du sensible*, Paris, La fabrique, 2000, p. 65.

early 1960s by the use of the term *joual* to designate the French language in Québec. But during the Quiet Revolution, a completely contemporary concept emerged – that of unilingualism[2] – which seemed to be even more fundamental to an assessment of the significance and newness of Québec's thinking about language. Before politically committed writers claimed *joual*, it was a purist variation on the worn-out theme of the deterioration of the popular language, whereas the idea of unilingualism, which had first appeared in the late

---

2. There is no official "definition" of Québec unilingualism : as I maintain further on, unilingualism is, first and foremost, an act of language, a means of resistance to bilingualism from within the language, and a slogan loud enough to have some chance of achieving political and ideological success. Thus, if union leader Michel Chartrand is to be believed, unilingualism is a vague, but powerful and effective concept indicating that French must be given priority in Québec : "*Bilingualism* translates *English*", he said, "*Unilingualism* translates *French*." (Michel CHARTRAND, cited by Susan PURCELL, "FQF is formed to battle Bill 63", *The Montreal Star*, October 27th 1969.)

1950s, bore with it the spark of a veritable revolution that was ideological, social and political.

Brandished like a banner during the Quiet Revolution, the idea of unilingualism was called into question at the same time as the great narrative of modern Québec[3], of which it formed an important part. Although not necessarily subjected to radical criticism, the idea is no longer espoused today as it was in the past, not even in the qualified form of "antinationalistic unilingualism" still advocated by essayist André Belleau in the early 1980s. That such a concept is a thing of the past is, in large part, only natural given the evolution and progress of Québec society. What is less natural, however, is the uneasiness denoted by the general silence about it. Permeating even

---

3. See Jocelyn LÉTOURNEAU, "Le 'Québec moderne' : un chapitre du grand récit collectif des Québécois", *Revue française de science politique*, vol. 42, n° 5, 1992, p. 765-785. Létourneau belongs to the new generation of historians striving to take some distance from the mythicizing of 1960s Québec.

the research community[4], this silence is no doubt primarily due to the fact that the "uni" (or "one") in "unilingualism" goes against the ideas and values embraced by Western societies in this highly modern era[5].

Yet such uneasiness indicates that we interpret "uni" in light of what it means in France in particular and in Europe as a whole[6]. Repeatedly criticized, the proffering of

---

4. There are indeed very few works on the specific issue of unilingualism (as distinct from the history, ideology and principles of the language legislation in Québec). It would nonetheless be worthwhile to consult Guy BOUTHILLIER, "Aux origines de la planification linguistique québécoise", in André MARTIN [ed.], *L'État et la planification linguistique II. Études de cas particuliers*, Québec, Éditeur officiel du Québec, 1981, p. 7-22 ; and Alain COMBRES, "La question linguistique et les partis politiques québécois (1960-1990)", Ph.D. diss, Université de Paris I, Panthéon-Sorbonne, 1996.

5. This point is illustrated in a special issue of the journal *Sociolinguistica* published in 1997. The title of the issue was trilingual and represented unilingualism as an ill to be remedied : *Einsprachigkeit ist heilbar/Monolingualism Is Curable/L'unilinguisme est curable.*

6. In fact, the sociolinguistic situation in Québec is very different from that in France : the "uni" in "unilingualism" is

unrestrained and sometimes self-interested interpretations, borrowed and applied without any qualification to America, let alone the minority context of Québec, has no merits in the field of intellectual and cultural history[7]. We must, however, go beyond such declarations of principle. Peculiarities on an epistemological level must be duly considered *in reality* and brought to bear in language itself as in research. "Unilingualism" is a very interesting case in point : the term ("unilinguisme") is used only in Québec[8] and does

---

not used primarily in reference to one unified language (as opposed to varieties of French), but rather to designate the unity and difference of one language in relation to another.

7. There are many examples of research and theories that take specific locations and national histories into account. Take, for instance, the term "intellectuel" (intellectual) ; a collective work recently published clearly shows very significant differences in the evolution of the term in England, France, Germany and Québec. See Michel LEYMARIE and Jean-François SIRINELLI [eds.], *L'histoire des intellectuels aujourd'hui*, Paris, Presses universitaires de France, 2003.

8. Except in rare situations ; it recently appeared in a work by French sociolinguist Henri Boyer, who was careful to

not appear in any of the main French-language dictionaries, except *Le Grand Robert*. However, the synonym "monolinguisme" ("monolingualism"), which has more neutral connotations, is commonly used in France and is listed in the dictionaries. In the final analysis, "unilingualism" designates a concept that is completely specific to the sociopolitical context of Québec. That is why the scope of the concept must be carefully delimited and defined.

"UNILINGUALISM":
A NEW WORD FOR A NEW POLICY

Despite the very long tradition of thinking about language in Québec, the idea of French

---

explain why he chose the term : "I use the word *unilingualism* (and not *monolingualism*) because I want to emphasize the result of a process that has tended to impose, most often through symbolic pressure […], uniqueness on two levels : the *inter*linguistic and the *intra*linguistic." (Free translation of "Ni concurrence, ni déviance : l'*unilinguisme* français dans ses œuvres", *Lengas*, vol. 48, 2000, p. 89.)

unilingualism did not emerge until the late 1950s. It was first introduced in 1958 by writer Jacques Ferron during a television appearance that he made while running as a left-wing candidate in the federal election. The idea received wider coverage the following year through Ferron – who revived it during the famous strike by Radio-Canada's Francophone producers – and the first separatist leaders, Raymond Barbeau and André d'Allemagne, who promoted it at that time. In 1961, the Rassemblement pour l'indépendance nationale (RIN), cofounded by d'Allemagne, included the idea in its platform ; given the party's visibility and success, the idea received credibility which quickly grew in the eyes of the public. The rapid acceptance of the idea raises the question as to why there was a strong need in neo-nationalist circles to forge a concept that was so new in comparison with the traditional positions of French Canada. To answer this question, it is essential to take a look at what, in the texts of the time, enabled unilingualism to gain favour with Quebecers and what, on an ideological level, gave substance and coherence to such a language planning project.

Careful examination of the gestation of unilingualism has revealed that the concept appeared after decades of bilingualism deemed to be as alienating in Québec as unachievable in the rest of Canada[9]. In this context, unilingualism constituted a rallying signal and the principle behind resistance led from within the language itself. It was the common name of a vision, practice and philosophy of language[10] that challenged the bilingualism

---

9. Karim LAROSE, "Unilinguisme de l'un, monolin-guisme de l'autre : langue et modernité au Québec" to appear in Ginette MICHAUD and Élisabeth NARDOUT-LAFARGE [eds.], *Construction de la modernité au Québec*, Outremont, Lanctôt, 2004, p. 119-135.

10. This philosophy of language could be referred to as "expressivism", as put forward by Charles Taylor. Since I am unable to elaborate here on this point, which is important to thinking about the emergence of unilingualism, I refer the reader to one of my previous works, which deals with the

actively promoted by the federal government, whose commitment to centralization was felt more intensely during the 1950s. Before being reflected almost two decades later in the *Charter of the French Language* (1977), unilingualism offered a place of recognition and of opposition to a language "policy" – a place where, according to Rancière, words shape a view of the world and impose an idea of things. Its appearance, then, had little or nothing to do with the monolingual obsession of large Western nations[11].

When the idea of unilingualism was launched by Jacques Ferron, the first discursive context in which it appeared was that of a political electoral battle (led in the name of socialism), followed by that of a union

---

contribution of this view of language to linguistic thinking in Québec : Karim LAROSE, *La langue de papier. Spéculations linguistiques au Québec (1957-1977)*, Montréal, Presses de l'Université de Montréal, 2004.

11. See Jacques DERRIDA, *Le monolinguisme de l'autre ou La prothèse d'origine*, Paris, Galilée, 1996.

conflict. In fact, the writer discussed his 1958 declaration on unilingualism for the first time in a text published in 1959 on the large-scale institutional struggle in Québec at the time : the strike by Radio-Canada producers[12]. Ferron was marked by the strike, as were many other intellectuals of the day, because of the total lack of solidarity the Canadian Broadcasting Corporation's English-speaking journalists showed their French-speaking colleagues. The Québec intelligentsia saw the strike as a betrayal of the main left-wing principles the newly-created dynamic corporation, representing the Canada of tomorrow, ordinarily and proudly upheld. They saw it as a sign that these principles worked in the end, i.e. in a time of crisis, along ethnic lines. A large number of intellectuals were compelled to denounce the difference in the treatment and status of Francophones as a distinct group.

---

12. Jacques FERRON, "Les racists" [*La Revue socialiste*, Spring 1959], *Escarmouches. La longue passe*, vol. 1, Montréal, Leméac, 1975, p. 21.

The primary impetus, then, for the unilingualism project, first formulated by Ferron – and not without with levity, irony and provocation – was profound disillusionment with the foundations of a "modern" Canada that were being laid with disregard for Québec. Historically, Québec had long believed in the merits of Canadian duality, particularly when it came to language. For decades, the most nationalistic Québec journal and one of the oldest, *L'Action nationale*, asked the federal administration and a number of the provincial governments that had prohibited or restricted the teaching of French in public schools, to implement real bilingualism that would do justice to the political project governing the foundation of Canada. For years, the French Canadian elite clamored for real bilingualism wherever numbers warranted, while there was still time. These demands, however, were never followed up with consistent initiatives by the federal government. Even the most liberal English-speaking intellectuals were reluctant to support the idea of widespread bilingualism in Canada through official policies. This was true, for example, of several English-speaking historians, whose reticence in this regard is clearly shown by Laurence Cros[13].

There is, in fact, a slightly more complex situation behind the conventional history of unilingualism, often associated with Québec nationalism. On a strictly chronological level, the term was first used to refer to *Anglophones'* knowledge and use of language. Before French-speaking intellectuals called for French unilingualism in Québec, they had expressed their disappointment on many occasions at being subjected to the systematic ignorance of French on the part of Canadian government employees, the English-speaking elite and Montréal merchants. Thus, English unilingualism was at issue, starting in about the

13. Laurence CROS, "Panorama de l'attitude des historiens anglophones canadiens vis-à-vis du bilinguisme", *Études canadiennes/Canadian Studies,* n° 45, 1998, p. 15-28.

1940s[14]. It was not by chance that the phenomenon, which grew with industrialization, was commented on more and more toward the late 1950s. Journalist Jean-Marc Léger, for example, indicated in 1958 that, given the deterioration of the situation, "English unilingualism would have to be prohibited on everything that reached the public[15]." The question was in no way one of imposing French unilingualism, but rather of preventing the language of the minority from becoming dominant with time.

As of the mid-1950s and during the 1960s, the Québec intelligentsia slowly and then radically abandoned the idea that equitable

---

14. See ANONYMOUS, "L'antibritannisme de l'unilinguisme" [proceedings of a talk by Charles Holmes titled *The Unbritishness of Unilingualism* criticizing the attitude of English Canadians toward French Canadians], *Le Devoir*, March 12th 1941.

15. Free translation of Jean-Marc LÉGER, "Blocs-notes. Le français, langue seconde au Québec ?" *Le Devoir*, August 7th 1958, p. 4.

bilingualism could be established in Canada. At the same time, it theorized about and implemented the French unilingualism project, created entirely in reaction to political events, to counter adverse unilingualism, which seemed to be guaranteed and masked by an unachievable ideal of bilingualism. The French unilingualism project thus emerged within a very specific ideological framework : at the dawn of the Quiet Revolution, when the dream of a French-speaking community from coast to coast was relinquished, intellectuals tried to outline, in the disorder, new perspectives for narrating the unity and singularity of Québec.

Ideas are rarely thought of in the abstract. More often, they are prompted by the imperatives of news and current events. The idea of unilingualism in Québec is no exception : it grew, first and foremost, out of the binary and divisive nature of bilingualism, i.e. out of a very specific polemical context. That being said, apart from the Canadian political discourse of the 1950s, there were at least three other ideological stepping stones that literally paved the way for reflection on and the implementation of unilingualism : the advent of neo-nationalist historiography in the 1950s[16], recourse to the principle of territoriality, and the legacy of conservative nationalism.

HISTORIOGRAPHY AND NEO-NATIONALISM

The emergence of the concept of unilingualism owes a great deal to new approaches in Québec historiography, particularly those put forward in the 1950s by a group of professors at the Université de Montréal's Institut d'histoire. Seeking to produce a global history that would take into account the unity of

---

16. It has been asserted that neo-nationalist historiography represented a break with the trends that preceded it ; although disputed by some historians, this assertion seems undeniable to me, given the originality of the *critical* approach devised by the École historique de Montréal.

French-Canadian society, academics such as Maurice Séguin, Michel Brunet and Guy Frégault played a major role in the evolution of attitudes toward language in Québec.

These three professors were strongly opposed to the traditionalist conception of French Canada, often colored by conservative, idealistic and somewhat messianic nationalism, and they felt a duty to veer in a new direction. They sought to compile an objective, realistic history that did not create any illusions by embellishing the past and fantasizing about the future. They intended to practice systematic doubt and, by drawing inspiration from the French École des Annales, to conceive of human history as an inextricably linked whole. In their view, political, economic and social phenomena had to be considered together[17]. They thought

---

17. Séguin asserts that "civil society or a community is an organism that is 'one', an organism of which the various aspects are integrally related." (Free translation of Maurice SÉGUIN as cited by Jean LAMARRE, *Le devenir de la nation*

it futile and artificial to contemplate only one of the many social forces that determine the evolution of Québec. All forces had to be equally examined, so that society would no longer be defined by its mission, spirit or soul, but rather as a "structure" in its entirety.

These neo-nationalist academics rejected the idea of confining historiographic work on French Canada to religion and culture. In so doing, they opened the door to greater emphasis on politics and economics. Their work differed from that of secular French-Canadian nationalists in tone or stress as well. While the watchword of traditionalist elites had been *survival*, that of neo-nationalists was *life*, full and complete. As a result, it is not difficult to understand why intellectuals in the 1950s reacted so strongly to the claim by well-known linguist, Pierre Daviault, that French was on the way to becoming a "dead language"

---

québécoise selon Maurice Séguin, Guy Frégault et Michel Brunet (1944-1969), Sillery, Septentrion, 1993, p. 150.)

in Québec. They denied the validity of this claim from the outset, assessed the situation over time, and then tried to remedy the language problem on the basis of priorities defined by the new historiography.

Toward the late 1950s, the influence of the École historique de Montréal grew in scope. Many intellectuals, tapping into neo-nationalist ideas, came to believe that, to give French a chance to live on, it was more realistic to concentrate development efforts and constructive measures within Québec territory than to disperse energies in defending a French-speaking community across Canada whose cause seemed increasingly hopeless without significant support from the federal government. This belief by the École de Montréal gave Québec symbolic unity and helped facilitate the emergence of the concept of unilingualism ; the first advocates of the concept based most of their arguments on neo-nationalist historiography.

They picked up, in particular, on the idea that, to change a situation affected by structural factors, a global view was essential. The idea of a single, all-encompassing vision was very much at work here. They felt that solutions should never be partial, because problems are global. This meant, for example, that the impact on the language, resulting from Québec's integration into the North American economy, could not be countered by organizing conferences on the language issue, speak-well competitions, and francization campaigns in the periodic press or by appealing to people to speak French in the name of some sort of daily heroism. According to these new intellectuals, only political State intervention could withstand such structural factors on a sustainable basis, and ensure that society remain a living principle, a place of action, and not a precarious space of mere survival.

RECOURSE TO THE PRINCIPLE
OF NATIONALITIES

Advocates of unilingualism also relied on the principle of nationalities – a fact that provides further insight into the language situation in the late 1950s. The principle first emerged in Europe during the first half of the 19th century. It claims to take into account the natural tendency of people to group together in a nation on the basis of their common history and language. It very quickly became the foundation of a liberation program for a number of oppressed nations (such as the Greeks under the Ottoman Empire). The principle of nationalities prevailed and gained recognition after the First World War when, on U.S. President Woodrow Wilson's initiative, it was used in redesigning the map of Europe. It is based on a very clear ideal of unity and is often summed up by the phrase, *one State, one nation, one language*, which should in theory coincide perfectly.

Inherent in the principle of nationalities is a desire for small nations to avoid domination considered foreign. It was very popular in the 1950s, especially during the African decolonization movement[18], from which Québec intellectuals drew enormous inspiration (the case of Algeria holding their attention, in

---

18. In fact, this movement refers more to the right of peoples to self-determination : "The nation has served among subordinated groups both as a defensive weapon employed to protect the group against external domination and as a sign of the unity, autonomy, and power of the community. During the period of de-colonialization and after, the nation appeared as the necessary vehicle for political modernization and hence the ineluctable path toward freedom and self-determination." (Micheal HARDT and Antonio NEGRI, *Empire*, Cambridge, Massachusetts, Harvard University Press, 2000, p. 132.) Stéphane PIERRÉ-CAPS, for his part, discusses the common origin of human rights and peoples'rights, and the tendency of observers to interpret the right to self-determination as a contemporary reformulation of the principle of nationalities, *Nations et peuples dans les constitutions modernes*, preface by François Borella, Nancy, Presses universitaires de Nancy, 1987, p. 494-496.

particular[19]). To give more weight to the idea of unilingualism, its promoters often cited the principle of nationalities[20], according to which in definable territories, aggregates of people who speak the same language should have full sovereignty over the territory in which they live in order to avoid relations of domination insofar as possible. The condition for their independence is unity. Thus, the singularity of communities is rooted in lan-

19. See Magali DELEUZE, *L'une et l'autre indépendance (1954-1964). Les médias au Québec et la guerre d'Algérie*, Montréal, Points de fuite, 2001.

20. See in particular Raymond BARBEAU, "Où va le Canada français ? L'exercice de la pleine souveraineté est essentiel à l'épanouissement du Québec", an interview by Jean-Marc LÉGER, *Le Devoir*, May 18th 1959 ; André D'ALLEMAGNE, "Le mythe du bilinguisme", *Laurentie*, no 106, September 1959, p. 352-353 ; Jacques FERRON, "Adieu au PSD" [*La Revue socialiste*, Summer 1960], in *Escarmouches. La longue passe*, p. 32 ; André D'ALLEMAGNE, *Le bilinguisme qui nous tue*, Montréal, Rassemblement pour l'indépendance nationale, c1962, p. 4 ; Raymond BARBEAU, *Le Québec bientôt unilingue ?*, Montréal, Éditions de l'Homme, 1965, p. 54.

guage[21]. The rationale for the principle tends to suggest that people can have only one language ; this, of course, would have the advantage of making their allegiance easy to identify, but is obviously a simplification of a much more complex situation.

An important nuance must be emphasized here. This principle was mentioned in most texts in Québec as an endorsement and reference on a theoretical level. There was no obsession with unity, since there was generally no question of challenging the existence of the Anglophone minority because it spoke a language different from the majority of the Québec nation which, it was believed, was to constitute a State whose official language

---

21. For d'Allemagne, "language is one of the main factors in the unity of a nation" and "it is in the context of language that nations are delimited." (Free translation of "Le mythe du bilinguisme", p. 350.) According to Barbeau as well, "language is a vital factor in the political and cultural unity of a nation." (Free translation of *Le Québec bientôt unilingue ?*, p. 19.)

would be French. This nuance explains why neo-nationalist intellectuals focused on the territorial aspect of the language issue and the principle of nationalities. In fact, what was advocated, albeit sometimes in slightly pompous terms, was only a *principle of territoriality* which, in Québec, does not yet have a name. The principle of territoriality, as applied in Belgium and Switzerland for example, provides that a specific language is associated with a distinct territory[22]. It can be considered a relatively apolitical variant of the principle of nationality since it does not, in itself, imply the constitution of a distinct State.

---

22. Canada and Québec hold opposing views in this respect, the former favoring the principle of personality (language right stems from individual rights) and the latter, the principle of territoriality (see Luisa DOMENICHELLI, "Comparaison entre les stratégies linguistiques de Belgique et du Canada", *Globe. Revue internationale d'études québécoises*, vol. 2, n° 2, 1999, p. 125-145).

HOMOGENEITY
AND RIGHT-WING UNILINGUALISM

The legacy of conservative nationalism, often characterized by an imperative of cultural homogeneity, also contributed, in its own way, to paving the way for the emergence of the idea of unilingualism. One of the very first separatists, Raymond Barbeau, was influenced by a long tradition of right-wing thinking, according to which "a religious melting pot [...] [was] as unacceptable as a cultural and language blend[23]." This marginal fraction of the intelligentsia, of which Barbeau was the best-known representative, upheld a cultural notion of nation rather than a civic one – which was not unusual at the time[24] – except

---

23. Free translation of *J'ai choisi l'indépendance*, Montréal, Éditions de l'Homme, 1961, p. 8.

24. Recent works on the idea of nation make it clear why care must be taken not to confuse the *cultural* notion of nation (based on the history of a community) with the *ethno-genealogical* one (based on strong organicism, rooted in the law of the blood, for example). It is also important not to be

that it was defined as entirely *one* and "culturally homogeneous[25]." The heritage of a long

---

fooled by the convenient opposition of cultural nation and
civic nation ; many theorists have shown the limitations and
imprecision of this opposition for more than a decade. The
works of Pierre Caussat, Marc Crépon and Anne-Marie
Thiesse are revealing in this regard.

25. "The proponents of the Canadian 'nation' have a geo-
graphic conception of nation ; they forget that a nation must
be culturally homogeneous, that spiritual and moral values
cannot withstand vagueness and permanent concession."
(Free translation of *ibid.*, p. 8.) The singularity of Barbeau's
ethno-nationalism is even clearer when it is compared with
that of the RIN and André d'Allemagne. For the RIN, "a
nation is essentially a historic and cultural community", but
is "pluralistic with its ethnic, social, political and religious
components, which unite in a common culture where new
contributions must assimilate." (Free translation of the *RIN
program*, adopted in October 1962 ; cited by André D'ALLE-
MAGNE, *Le RIN de 1960 à 1963. Étude d'un groupe de pression
au Québec*, preface by Marcel Rioux, Montréal, L'Étincelle,
1974, p. 41.) Although a form of unity or pooling is necessary,
it does not preclude pluralism. D'Allemagne chose to over-
look "ethnic nationalism" based on blood and race, but
believed that a nation cannot exist without a form of unity.
"A product of history", culture has the federating function of
the "mould" in which the various "collective activities" of a
people combine ; such culture is continuously being built, as

inward-looking past, this position was toned down, even by the most radical, as the 1960s wore on. Yet it suggests how unilingualism, based on a concern for social justice by most, could be exploited from an ethnocentric perspective by some. Thus the importance of paying careful attention to the details, nuances, history and spirit of such a concept.

Raymond Barbeau, for his part, maintained essentially the same definition of nation throughout the years, i.e. "homogeneity of ethnicity, language, religion, history and traditions, exclusive possession of a territory, collective will to live, in a word, complete national unity[26]." While the "ethnic" aspect does not indicate any racism here, it certainly implies a collective sharing of experiences and

---

the history of a nation is an ongoing, never-ending process (André d'ALLEMAGNE, *Le colonialisme au Québec*, Montréal, Éditions R-B, 1966, p. 79 and 111.)

26. Free translation of Raymond BARBEAU, "M. Raymond Barbeau" [response to a survey on nationalism], *Tradition et progrès*, vol. 2, n° 2, December 1958-March 1959, p. 12.

values that tends to exclude anyone wishing to be integrated into the nation. Barbeau emphasized unity and cohesion much more than reception and integration. He was not xenophobic, but rather totally indifferent to the need to consider contact with others in terms of hospitality. In this type of discourse, homogeneity must be seen as one of the features of unity. As one of the principles of right-wing nationalism, it occasionally served as a basis for reflecting on the language.

Representing the conservative fraction of thinking about unilingualism, the intellectuals who used the term *homogeneity* infused it with an ideal of a collective identity obsessed with boundaries and borders : they saw "unilingualism as the normal and natural condition of a unified people[27]." This attitude, however, was not predominant among

---

27. Free translation of Raymond BARBEAU, "En marge de la Commission Laurendeau-Dunton. L'imposture du bilinguisme et la nécessité de l'unilinguisme", *Revue annuelle de la Société du Bon Parler français*, May 1964, p. 14.

advocates of unilingualism; on the contrary, it was maintained only by Raymond Barbeau, his circle and certain marginal right-wing publications with limited distribution.

FROM UNILINGUALISM TO THE
CHARTER OF THE FRENCH LANGUAGE

Although the unilingualism project – formulated in different ways in recent decades[28] – has marked the history of thinking about language in Québec, it may not offer the best key to understanding the issues involved in the *Charter of the French Language* (Bill 101). Unilingualism was certainly a catalyst for the rejection of veiled bilingualism, thus

---

28. Before Bill 101 was passed, there were at least four variants of the unilingualism project: 1. that of the first sovereignists, still sketchy (1958-1965); 2. that of the RIN, which was developed in particular when the organization became a political party (1965-1968); 3. that of the Parti québécois, more moderate (1968-1977); 4. that of Société Saint-Jean-Baptiste and its network. Each of these variants evolved and was marked by specific refusals and priorities.

enabling Québec intellectuals to start thinking about practical solutions to the language problems in Québec. Many of these solutions, although not all, were modified and used in the different language laws adopted, but the idea of "uni" or "one", which had served within and through the language to galvanize energies around the *word* "unilingualism" at the beginning of the 1960s, was no longer necessary and fell by the wayside. Thus, despite certain ambiguities, Bill 101 cannot in any way be defined by the will to impose French and eliminate language diversity in Québec like the language homogenization process implemented in France beginning in the 18th century. This undoubtedly is the main reason the word "unilingualism", considered too radical, disappeared for all intents and purposes from contemporary thinking about language in Québec.

Practically speaking, the *Charter of the French Language* has one objective : to enable the French-speaking majority to "live in their language[29]." *To live* must be interpreted in the fullest sense of the word. *To live* means to work, to express oneself, to communicate without language being a daily, exhausting and humiliating struggle. All the different Québec political parties, from the Liberal Party to the Union nationale, have agreed on this point, differing only in their perceptions of what *to live* means on a social level. For the separatists, this was a crucial issue that had to be taken seriously. Not only did they have a very noble idea of what every speaker should be entitled to in terms of language, but they wanted to put that ideal into practice. By basing themselves on a sociolinguistic analysis of the situation, they believed that, for French to be a living language, it had to be clearly

---

29. Michel PLOURDE, "La Charte de la langue française du Québec", *La langue française au Québec. Conférences et allocutions (1980-1985)*, Conseil de la langue française, Éditeur officiel du Québec, 1985, p. 18-19.

defined as the "common language"[30] of Quebecers and there was no room for any ambiguity in that respect.

If there is a logic to the "one" in Bill 101, it is to be found in the qualifier "common" or "as one", i.e. in a vision of the language as common property that would bring all of Québec society together. To take this logic farther, for French to assert itself as the language shared by all Quebecers, the commitment for it had to be written into legislation, since nothing on an economic level would enable it to live on as a natural given. It was thus necessary to give French clear priority and to reject the principle of official bilingualism. This does not prevent, it must be repeated, the two languages from coexisting in reality or

30. Camille LAURIN, "Allocution prononcée devant le Canadian Club de Montréal" [1977], *Le français, langue du Québec*, Éditions du Jour, 1977, p. 30. See also Camille LAURIN, "Québec bilingue ou Québec français" [1992], *Une traversée du Québec*, preface by Jacques Parizeau, Montréal, L'Hexagone, 1999, p. 91.

institutional bilingualism from being alive and well (but that is not the question). Such a rejection of official bilingualism has symbolic significance that strengthens the position of French without threatening that of English (which is thriving with a language community of more than 300 million speakers and does not need official recognition or protection to survive and live on).

Since defending the equality of the languages in Québec served to perpetuate the supremacy of English, the issue was not one of making the second language disappear, but rather of ensuring that the language of the minority ceased to dominate the sociolinguistic arena at the expense of that of the majority. The father of the *Charter of the French Language*, Camille Laurin, claimed consistently that the bill enacted by his party was in the spirit of the white paper on culture, which had been prepared by a Parti québécois opponent, Pierre Laporte, a Liberal Party minister, who was already promoting the "priority" of the French language in 1965[31].

As journalist Graham Fraser observed, "bilingualism – which gave official and equal status to French and English, thus diminishing the symbolic importance of French and giving English recognition as a common language for non-francophones – was to be explicitly rejected[32]." This meant that a number of measures with real social impact had to be adopted. Accordingly, the *Charter* declares that French is not only the official language, but also the language of the State, education, work and business in Québec. In line with the Liberal Party on this point as well, the *Charter* aimed

---

31. Camille LAURIN, "Allocution devant l'Association des manufacturiers canadiens" [1977], *Le français, langue du Québec*, p. 49. This commitment by the Liberal Party was reaffirmed during the 1966 election. In 1968, Union nationale leader Daniel Johnson also stated that French should have the same status as English in Ontario and thus become the prevailing language in Québec.

32. Graham FRASER, *P.Q. : Réné Lévesque and the Parti québécois in Power*, Toronto, Macmillan of Canada, 1984, p. 100.

to ensure that French would *effectively* become the first language in Québec.

Journalist Jacques Keable best expressed the language balance that Québec was seeking to achieve and that Bill 101 has tried to implement. He anticipated that the report by the Gendron Commission of Inquiry on the Position of the French Language in Québec, when tabled in 1972, would recommend that

> French [be], *if not the only legal language, the only mandatory language in virtually all communication other than personal in Québec. As a result, English* [...] [would] *lose its equal status and assume the fairer position of non-mandatory second language, while maintaining its legal value*[33].

This passage is interesting in that it puts the Québec language problem in the proper perspective and reverses the way in which it has all too often had to be broached.

---

33. December 26th 1971, p. 4.

In light of the evolution of thinking about language in Québec, it indeed seems erroneous to attribute unilingualism to the *Charter of the French Language*. In the *Charter*, what is important, once again, is not the idea of unity, but the will for communication to be in French, the language of the majority, and for French to be at the heart of social life in Québec. Nothing more, nothing less. French could not develop if it continued to be swallowed up by English, the dominant language in North America, which imposed itself as a result of its socioeconomic prestige. By picking up on the ideas that grew out of the unilingualism project and rejecting any exclusivist approach, the *Charter of the French Language*, changes this state of affairs by reaffirming, in the name of language expressivism intended to give speakers back their full dignity, that French must remain a *living* language and that, for it to do so, it must become the *common* language, *first* language and therefore the *official* language in all the main areas of life in society.

FRENCH AS
THE "COMMON PUBLIC LANGUAGE"
IN QUÉBEC[1]

Leigh Oakes

It's official : French in Québec is no longer the sole property of the French Canadian ethnic

1. This article is an abridged and modified version of Leigh OAKES, "French – a language for everyone in Québec ?", *Nations and Nationalism*, vol. 10, n° 4, p. 539-558 (Permission granted by the editors of *Nations and Nationalism*, Journal of the Association for the Study of Ethnicity and Nationalism, London School of Economics). I wish to thank Jane Warren, Gérard Bouchard, Claude Verreault, Céline Gagnon and Bill Marshall for their comments on the issues raised herein, as well as the Arts and Humanities Research Board (AHRB) for its financial support. All translations from the French are mine.

group[2]. According to the report of the *Commission des États généraux sur la situation et l'avenir de la*

---

2. Following Gérard Bouchard, ethnic identity is defined here in a broad sense, which implies a significant degree of overlap with cultural identity (Gérard BOUCHARD, "Ouvrir le cercle de la nation. Activer la cohésion sociale. Réflexion sur le Québec et sa diversité", *L'Action nationale*, vol. 87, n° 4, 1997, p. 128). It is nonetheless clearly distinguished from the latter, especially because of the myth of common origin, the *"sine qua non* of ethnicity" (Anthony D. SMITH, *The Ethnic Origins of Nations*, Oxford, Blackwell, 1986, p. 24). For further discussions on the important differences between ethnicity and culture, see Thomas Hylland ERIKSEN, *Ethnicity and Nationalism*, London, Pluto Press, 1993, p. 33-35 and Ross POOLE, *Nation and Identity*, London, Routledge, 1999, p. 39. With the decline of the concept of "French Canada", some prefer to refer to the ethnic majority in Québec as "Quebecers of French Canadian heritage" (Jocelyn LÉTOUR-NEAU, "Penser le Québec (dans le paysage canadien)", Michel VENNE [ed.], *Penser la nation québécoise*, Montréal, Le Devoir et Québec/Amérique, coll. "Débats", 2000, p. 107), or "Franco-Quebecers" (Gérard BOUCHARD, "Construire la nation québécoise. Manifeste pour une coalition nationale", Michel VENNE [éd.], *Penser la nation québécoise*, Montréal, Le Devoir et Québec/Amérique, coll. "Débats", 2000, p. 54). Following Danielle Juteau, the expression adopted here is nonetheless "French Canadian", while it is recognized that the French Canadians of former times are not the same as

langue française au Québec, otherwise known as the Larose Commission, French now belongs to all ethnic groups in Québec; it has become "a language for everyone[3]". These are fine words, but what is the real intention of such a declaration and what are its implications ?

To be sure, French has made considerable progress since the adoption of the Charter of the French Language in 1977[4]. According to a study commissioned by the *Conseil de la langue française*, 87 % of Québec's population in 1997 had French as its main *"langue d'usage public"*

---

their descendants : "Since ethnicity constantly transforms itself, the French Canadian ethnicity of yesterday and that of today are very different from each other" (Danielle JUTEAU, "Le défi de l'option pluraliste", Michel VENNE [éd.], *Penser la nation québécoise*, Montréal, Le Devoir et Québec/Amérique, coll. "Débats", 2000, p. 211).

3. GOUVERNEMENT DU QUÉBEC, *Le français, une langue pour tout le monde. (Rapport de la Commission des États généraux sur la situation de l'avenir de la langue française au Québec)*, Québec, Gouvernement du Québec, 2001.

4. Marc LEVINE, *La reconquête de Montréal*, Montréal, VLB éditeur, 1997.

(language of public use)[5]. However, the idea that French constitutes a language of public use for *all* Quebecers, or what has become known as a "*langue publique commune*" (common public language), is more than a simple means of describing a sociolinguistic phenomenon ; more importantly, it is a political device which forms part of a broader project of redefining the Québécois nation in more inclusive, non-ethnic terms.

Despite the optimistic discourse of the authorities and certain intellectuals, two issues in particular still need to be resolved : can a language really be completely "de-ethnicized" as some suggest ? And how can new Quebecers be motivated to adopt for their public communications a language that has traditionally been associated with French Canadian ethnicity ? Before examining these questions in more detail, it is appropriate to consider briefly the history of the concept of *langue publique commune* as it is used in Québec.

---

5. Paul BÉLAND, *Le français, langue d'usage public au Québec en 1997. Rapport de recherche*, Québec, Conseil de la langue française, 1999.

HISTORY OF FRENCH
AS THE LANGUE PUBLIQUE COMMUNE

Ever since the 1960s-1970s, the idea has frequently been raised of making French the *langue commune* of Québec. For example, the *Commission d'enquête sur la situation du français et sur les droits linguistiques*, also called the Gendron Commission, declared that :

> [w]e recommend that the Government of Québec sets itself the general objective of making French the common language of Quebecers, that is, the language which, known by all, can serve as an instrument of communication in contact situations between French-speaking and non-French-speaking Quebecers[6].

---

6. GOUVERNEMENT DU QUÉBEC, *La situation de la langue française au Québec. Rapport de la commission d'enquête sur la situation de la langue française et sur les droits linguistiques au Québec. Livre I. La langue de travail : la situation du français dans les activités de travail et de consommation des Québécois,* Québec, Gouvernement du Québec, 1972, p. 154.

Five years later, the same assertion was made in the White Paper that was to lead to the Charter of the French Language. Its author, the Minister for Cultural Development, Camille Laurin, was careful to distinguish this policy from linguistic assimilation.

> *The total assimilation of all new immigrants, to the extent that they have lost all ties to their country of origin within one or two generations, is not a desirable objective. A society that allows its minority groups to maintain their language and culture is a society that is richer and probably better balanced*[7].

Even if it was not intended to be assimilationist, the policy of promoting French as the *langue commune* of Québec as it existed at the time did, however, form part of a broader policy of *culture de convergence* according to which non-French

7. Gouvernement du Québec, *La politique québécoise de la langue française*, Québec, Gouvernement du Québec, 1977, p. 26.

speakers were encouraged to "converge" towards the culture of the French-speaking ethnic majority. The main architect of this *culture de convergence* policy was Fernard Dumont. It is therefore of no surprise that, in his capacity as Deputy Minister for Cultural Development, Dumont was also one of the co-signatories of the 1977 White Paper[8].

By the 1990s, the idea of convergence behind French as the *langue commune* of Québec had all but disappeared. The new concern of liberal democracies for cultural diversity now made it necessary to state explicitly that new Quebecers had the right to speak the language of their choice in the private sphere. To recognize that the requirement that they adopt French was indeed limited to the public sphere, reference was no longer made to French as the *langue commune*, but rather as the *langue publique commune*. This "publicization" of the concept of *langue commune* is clearly manifested in official documents of the time.

---

8. Geneviève MATHIEU, *Qui est Québécois ? Synthèse du débat sur la redéfinition de la nation*, Montréal, VLB éditeur, 2001, p. 18-19.

> *This valorisation of French as the common language and language of public life does not, however, mean that one should confuse the mastering of a common language with linguistic assimilation. Indeed, as a democratic society, Québec respects the right of individuals to adopt the language of their choice in communications of a private nature[9].*

In 1996, the *Comité interministériel sur la situation de la langue française* sought to consolidate this "new definition of the linguistic integration process[10]" based on the common public language. While the traditional categories used in censuses of the time were *langue maternelle* (mother tongue) and *langue d'usage* (the language spoken at home), the *Comité* favored an approach which would put more emphasis on the language used in the public

---

9. GOUVERNEMENT DU QUÉBEC, *Au Québec, pour bâtir ensemble. Énoncé de politique en matière d'immigration et d'intégration*, Québec, Ministère des Communautés culturelles et de l'Immigration, 1990.

10. Marc LEVINE, *op. cit.*, p. 361.

sphere, thus allowing for a better evaluation of the aims of the Charter of the French language.

> *In order to determine whether French has progressed as the "normal and everyday language" of public activities in Québec, one can evidently not rely on data relating to the* langue maternelle; *at the same time, it is not obvious that one should limit oneself to data regarding the* langue d'usage, *since the language spoken at home is not necessarily the language used at work or in public communications. Consequently, it is clear that one should use data relating to the* langue commune *(or civic language), but these data are not yet available. This can therefore lead to an underestimation of the number of "Quebecers speaking French", especially amongst allophones (if they use French in their public communications more than at home*[11]*).*

---

11. GOUVERNEMENT DU QUÉBEC, *Le français langue commune. Enjeu de la société québécoise. (Rapport du comité interministériel sur la situation de la langue française)*, Québec, Gouvernement du Québec, 1996, p. 10.

For this reason, the *Comité* introduced the notion of *langue d'usage public* and called for the creation of a real instrument of measurement for this new concept. In 1997, a study was therefore carried out "to evaluate the public use of languages and devise a global index[12]". An *indicateur des langues d'usage public* (index of languages of public use) was constructed using statistical information concerning the use of languages in a dozen domains of activity : in shops, at the bank, in the workplace, when using public services, etc. As the *Comité* had hoped, the new index has resulted in more positive statistics : whereas only 83 % of Québec's population claim to speak French in the home, 87 % declare it as their main *langue d'usage public* (see table 1).

---

12. Paul BÉLAND, *op. cit.*, p. 4.

Table 1.
Percentage of the population according to mother tongue, the language spoken at home and the language of public use (index) in the whole of Québec in 1997. The population was 18 years or older and native or immigrated before 1995, and was required to declare one mother tongue only. N=13,295[13].

	LANGUAGE CATEGORY			
LANGUAGE	MOTHER TONGUE	LANGUAGE SPOKEN AT HOME	LANGUAGE OF PUBLIC USE	MAIN LANGUAGE OF PUBLIC USE
FRENCH	82	83	82	87
FRENCH AND ENGLISH	N/A	1	8	N/A
ENGLISH	8	10	8	11
OTHER	9	6	1	1

It must be noted that the *indicateur des langues d'usage public* has received much criticism, especially by statisticians and demographers, who

_____

13. Paul BÉLAND, *op. cit.*, p. 46.

claim that its "*faux-fuyant*" ("red herring") or "chimerical" nature conceals the actual precarious position of the French language, especially on the island of Montréal[14]. The methodological procedures used in the 1997 study have also been subject to rigorous criticism[15]. Nonetheless, as a political device, the notion of *langue d'usage public* seems to be on the way to replacing *transfert linguistique* (language shift or instance thereof), which implies a certain degree of assimilation from which the authorities are keen to distance themselves.

More recently, the concept of *langue publique commune* has found its place as an essential

---

14. Charles CASTONGUAY, "Et la langue de travail, monsieur Larose ?", Charles Castonguay, Pierre Dubuc and Jean-Claude Germain, *Larose n'est pas Larousse. Regards critiques – la Commission des États généraux sur la situation et l'avenir de la langue française au Québec*, Paroisse Notre-Dame-des-Neiges, Éditions Trois-Pistoles and Montréal, Éditions du Renouveau québécois, 2002, p. 13.

15. Christian ROY, "L'usage des langues dans la sphère publique au Québec", *Bulletin d'histoire politique*, vol. 10, n° 1, 2001, p. 151-160.

element in the new, citizen-orientated conception of Québécois identity. For example, it featured prominently in the submissions presented to the *Commission des États généraux sur la situation et l'avenir de la langue française au Québec*; it was also one of the key concepts of the Commission's report itself.

> *All persons living in the territory of Québec, whatever their origin, receive* en partage *the official and common language of Québec. French thus becomes the privileged means of access to the civic heritage (values, rights, obligations, institutions, etc.) common to all Quebecers and on which their citizenship is founded. The French language offers a site for the exploration and development of the values peculiar to the whole of Québécois society. It is also the site of a* vouloir-vivre collectif, *the common public space where everyone can meet*[16].

16. GOUVERNEMENT DU QUÉBEC, *Le français, une langue pour tout le monde*, p. 13. Even if the Commission makes reference predominantly to French as the *langue commune*, it is understood that this implies *langue publique commune*.

French as the *langue publique commune* is thus seen as the key to civic participation, to one's citizenship. It is a means of maintaining the social cohesion of the ethnically diverse society that is Québec in the twenty-first century. To take these new aspirations for French into account, the Commission favored a move away from the language policy of the past that was based on the *survivance* of the majority ethnic group. To this effect, it recommended :

> [t]*hat language policy in Québec definitively depart from the historical, Canadian approach which divides Québécois identity along ethnic lines – French Canadian and English Canadian – and replace it with a civic approach which bases the identity of the people of Québec on reception and inclusion with the help of a* langue commune

Indeed, the definition given for the former is : "In Québec, the normal and everyday language used by all citizens in their daily communications, excluding those of a private nature and those exceptions for which the Charter of the French Language provides", *ibid.*, p. 225.

*formed by the contribution of all constit-
uent parts*[17].

The notion of *langue publique commune* has
also figured prominently in the debate among
academics about which model of nation will best
express the ethnic diversity of Québec today. For
example, Diane Lamoureux believes that it is
essential to dissociate language and culture : she
asserts that French in Québec should be considered as a mere means of communication, and not
as the bearer of the French Canadian cultural
memory[18]. Similarly, as part of his model of
nation for Québec based on republican values and
Habermas' theory of constitutional patriotism,
Claude Bariteau insists that "[i]n a political project in a multicultural environment, it is important not to link language and cultural belonging[19]."

17. *Ibid.*, p. 21.

18. Diane LAMOUREUX, "L'autodétermination comme
condition du multiculturalisme québécois", *Politique et sociétés*, n° 28, automne 1995, p. 53-69.

19. Claude BARITEAU, *Québec 18 septembre 2001. Le monde
pour horizon*, Montréal, Québec/Amérique, coll. "Débats",
1998, p. 163.

These comments lead us to make an important observation : even civic nationalisms make use of language as a symbol of national identity, but by emphasising a different function. While for ethnic nationalisms, language unites those with the same mythical ancestry, for civic nationalisms, the dissociation of language and ethnicity is seen as the best way to unify an ethnically diverse society, to bring the different components together into what Anderson would call an "imagined community". Indeed, Anderson claims that :

> [l]*anguage is not an instrument of exclusion : in principle, anyone can learn any language. On the contrary, it is fundamentally inclusive, limited only by the fatality of Babel : no one lives long enough to learn all languages*[20].

Similarly, Manuell Castells hypothesises that :

---

20. Benedict ANDERSON, *Imagined Communities : Reflections on the Origin and Growth of Nationalism,* London, Verso, 1983, p. 122.

> *language, and particularly a fully developed*
> *language, is a fundamental attribute of self-*
> *recognition, and of the establishment of an*
> *invisible national boundary less arbitrary*
> *than territoriality, and* less exclusive than
> ethnicity [emphasis added][21].

Castells is partially referring to Catalonia, where increased immigration both from other regions of Spain and the Maghrebi countries in particular, coupled with a falling birth rate amongst indigenous Catalans, has provoked authorities to attempt to dissociate language and Catalan identity.

> *Too much insistence on that bond is likely to*
> *alienate those whose first language is not*
> *Catalan, and it may encourage them to*
> *insist that their linguistic rights take*
> *precedence over Catalan self-ascription*[22].

21. Manuel CASTELLS, *The Power of Identity*, Oxford, Blackwell Publishers, 1997, p. 52.

22. Charlotte HOFFMANN, "Balancing language planning and language rights : Catalonia's uneasy juggling act", *Journal of Multilingual and Multicultural Development*, vol. 21, n° 5, 2000, p. 435.

Encouraging immigrants to associate with and participate in the wider society is an obvious concern for the authorities in Québec as well, especially considering the low birth rates amongst native French speakers. But can language be dissociated from ethnic identity in this way ? Can language be completely "de-ethnicized" as the Québec authorities and certain intellectuals seem to want ?

CAN LANGUAGE BE "DE-ETHNICIZED" ?

Already in 1988, Raymond Breton predicted that the presence of immigrants in Québec would result in the "the progressive dissociation of language from ethnicity[23]". Fifteen years on, we are now in a better position to evaluate these predictions. It is true that, even if he or she will never be able to become a *Canadien français* (an ethnic French Canadian), the child of immigrant to

---

23. Raymond BRETON, "From ethnic to civic nationalism : English Canada and Québec", *Ethnic and Racial Studies*, vol. 11, n° 1, 1988, p. 97-98.

Québec can nonetheless participate in Québécois society by becoming a *francophone*[24]. But the use of language, as opposed to ethnicity, as a parameter of social categorisation by no means weakens the link between these two concepts. As Guy Bouthillier points out, "[t]he majority of ethnic groups have the right to their [own] *phone* : italophone, hellenophone, hispanophone, not forgetting creolophone[25]."

Moreover, the term *francophone* demands closer attention. A survey of dictionaries of Québécois French shows that, when defining this word, a broad, "international" perspective is usually adopted. For example, the *Dictionnaire du français plus à l'usage des francophones d'Amérique* describes a francophone as "[f]or whom French is the mother or official language[26]", the *Dictionnaire*

24. Gérard BOUCHARD, "Construire la nation québécoise. Manifeste pour une coalition nationale", p. 59.

25. Guy BOUTHILLIER, *L'obsession ethnique*, Montréal, Lanctôt éditeur, 1997, p. 84.

26. *Dictionnaire du français plus à l'usage des francophones d'Amérique,* edition established under the responsibility of

québécois d'aujourd'hui as "[w]ho speaks French, either as a mother, official or second language[27]" and the most recent *Dictionnaire québécois-français* simply as a *"pers*[onne] *de langue française*[28]" ("French speaker"). However, anyone spending time in Québec will notice that the word is often used to describe an ethnic, rather than purely linguistic reality. For example, the above definitions undeniably include immigrants from France, yet the latter are usually referred to as *Français* and not *francophones*, a term by and large reserved for those of French Canadian descent[29]. Even within

A. E. Shiaty, with the collaboration of Pierre Auger and Normand Beauchemin ; principal editor : Claude Poirier, with the assistance of Louis Mercier and Claude Verreault, Montréal, Centre Éducatif et Culturel inc, 1988, p. 706.

27. *Dictionnaire québécois d'aujourd'hui*, edited by Jean-Claude Boulanger ; supervised by Alain Rey, Saint Laurent, Dicorobert inc, 1992, p. 513-514.

28. Lionel Meney, *Dictionnaire québécois-français*, Montréal, Guérin, 1999, p. 864.

29. In a similar manner, the French have a propensity to exclude themselves from the term francophone, which they tend to reserve for French speakers from countries other than France (Bernhard Pöll, *Francophonies périphériques : histoire,*

official and academic circles, where in theory everyone using French in the public sphere is francophone, reference needs on occasion to be made to the *francophones de souche*[30] (i.e. those with French as a mother tongue). If the new approach is to emphasise French as the *langue publique commune*, why are these distinctions still made ?

The answer to this question can be found in theories of intergroup relations within the field of social psychology. According social identity theory, for example, all individuals have a fundamental need to distinguish themselves from others, to attain psychological distinctiveness, in this case on an ethnic dimension[31]. In other words, ethnicity is

statut et profil des principales variétés du français hors de France, Paris, L'Harmattan, 2001, p. 21-22).

30. See, for example, Gérard BOUCHARD, *La nation québécoise au futur et au passé*, Montréal, VLB éditeur, 1999, p. 69, 77.

31. Henri TAJFEL, "Social identity and intergroup behaviour", *Social Science Information*, vol. 13, 1974, p. 65-93 ; Henri TAJFEL, *The Social Psychology of Minorities. (Minority Rights Group Report 38)*, London, Minority Rights Group, 1978 ; Henri TAJFEL and John C. TURNER, "The social identity theory of intergroup behaviour", in Stephen WORCHEL and

indeed exclusive, in so far as social identities are invariably constructed in contradistinction to others. This is not to imply, however, that an individual cannot assimilate to the majority group if so desired, no more than it hinders different ethnic groups from living as equals in the same society or nation, depending on how the latter is defined. As Gérard Bouchard reminds us, ethnicity should not be confused with ethnocentrism or ethnicism[32]. It is these phenomena which should be condemned, and not ethnicity itself, because they invariably drive individuals to discriminate against members of other ethnic groups, irrespective of how much a common culture and language are promoted.

In France, for example, despite the much vaunted republican model, ethnic discrimination manifested through language still exists. About the French spoken by foreigners, Julia Kristeva observes that :

William G. AUSTIN [eds.], *Psychology of Intergroup Relations*, 1986, revised edition of *The Social Psychology of Intergroup Relations*, Chicago, Nelson-Hall Publishers, 1979.

32. Gérard BOUCHARD, *La nation québécoise au futur et au passé*, p. 30.

> [e]*ven when he is legally and adminis-*
> *tratively accepted, the foreigner is not for all*
> *that accepted into* [French] *families. His*
> *untoward usage of the French language*
> *discredits him, consciously or not, in the*
> *eyes of the natives who identify themselves*
> *more than in other countries with their*
> *polished and cherished speech*[33].

Liliane Vassberg confirms this observation, this time about a variety of French indigenous to France, notably Alsatian French.

> [A]*n Alsatian accent when pronouncing*
> *French usually produces very negative judg-*
> *ments of the speaker : "an accent" is consi-*
> *dered unrefined, ungraceful, crude, ridicu-*
> *lous, a mark of lower-class origins and a*
> *lack of education*[34].

33. Julia KRISTEVA, *Étrangers à nous-mêmes*, Paris, Fayard, 1988, p. 58.
34. Liliane M. VASSBERG, *Alsatian Acts of Identity : Language Use and Language Attitudes in Alsace*, Clevedon, Multilingual Matters, 1993, p. 170.

Using the "matched-guise" technique, John Paltrige and Howard Giles also found that a Parisian accent was rated more favorably than an Provençal one, which itself was considered more prestigious than a Breton accent, which itself was judged more positively than an Alsatian accent[35]. Empirical research has shown that "evaluations of language varieties [such as these] do not reflect intrinsic linguistic or aesthetic qualities so much as the levels of status and prestige that they are *conventionally* associated with in particular speech communities[36]". In other

35. John PALTRIDGE and Howard GILES, "Attitudes towards speakers of regional accents of French : Effects of regionality, age and sex of listeners", *Linguistische Berichte*, vol. 90, 1984, p. 71-85. The "matched-guise" technique is used to elicit attitudes towards speakers of different languages of varieties of language. It consists of playing to a target group recordings of a passage read by a single person in different languages or accents. Members of the target group then have to evaluate what they believe to be different speakers using a scale corresponding to degrees of friendliness, sincerity, intelligence, trustworthiness, etc.

36. Howard GILES and Nikolas COUPLAND, *Language : Contexts and Consequences*, Milton Keynes, Open University Press, 1991, p. 37-38.

words, negative opinions about different varieties of French express negative views about the ethnic groups that speak them.

There is also the example of the English Only movement in the United States. Calls heard since the middle of the 1980s by associations such as US English to make English the official language of individual states, as well as at the federal level, are the product of ethnicism or what is termed in the US, the "new nativism[37]". Similarly in Sweden, where nationalist rhetoric has been played down since the 1930s, language offers a means of discrimination against immigrants which is more "politically correct" than race or ethnicity[38]. Such

37. Geoffrey NUNBERG, "Lingo Jingo : English Only and the New Nativism", *The American Prospect*, vol. 8, n° 33, 1997, http://www.prospect.org/print-friendly/print/V8/33/nunberg-g.html (April 17th 2000) ; Carol L. SCHMID, *The Politics of Language : Conflict, Identity, and Cultural Pluralism in Comparative Perspective*, New York, Oxford University Press, 2001, p. 41-43.

38. Leigh OAKES, *Language and National Identity : Comparing France and Sweden*, Amsterdam and Philadelphia, John Benjamins, 2001, p. 114-115.

behaviour serves as evidence against Anderson's claim mentioned above, that language is not an instrument of exclusion.

Even leaving aside this ethnicism played out through language, it must be noted that language is nonetheless associated with ethnicity in more banal situations. As Will Kymlicka shows using the example of the US, so-called civic nations are in fact not as ethnoculturally neutral as they think[39]. In France, too, the choice of French as a common public language is far from ethnoculturally neutral. Speakers of minority languages have long fought for official recognition of their languages, but this has been consistently rejected[40]. When supporters of the republican model of integration vehemently reject what they refer to as "the 'ethnicization' of public life[41]", they neglect the fact that

---

39. Will KYMLICKA, *Politics in the Vernacular : Nationalism, Multiculturalism and Citizenship*, Oxford, Oxford University Press, 2001, p. 24-25.

40. Leigh OAKES, *op. cit.*, p. 121-124.

41. Dominique SCHNAPPER, *La communauté des citoyens. Sur l'idée de nation*, Paris, Gallimard, 1994, p. 98.

the public sphere in France is already founded on the ethnic identity of the dominant core. In the words of Michel Seymour, "Jacobin Republicans who relentlessly denounce minority claims are most often unconscious nationalists[42]." In Canada as well, despite the much vaunted model of multiculturalism, it is often forgotten that "there is no mosaic without cement, [and] in this case, it is English Canada which is the cement[43]". In what is termed the "liberal paradox[44]", the civic nation often denies the communitarian base on which it is built. This has the effect of further discrediting the concept of ethnicity, by reinforcing the fallacy that only minorities have ethnic identities.

---

42. Michel SEYMOUR, "Le libéralisme, la politique de la reconnaissance, et le cas du Québec", in Will KYMLICKA [ed.], *Comprendre*, vol. 1, n° 1, http://mapageweb.umontreal.ca/lepagef/dept/cahiers/Seymour_liberalisme.pdf, p. 5 (November 7th 2002).

43. Guy BOUTHILLIER, *op. cit.*, p. 188.

44. *Ibid.*, p. 2.

Eriksen also notes the impossibility of dissociating language and ethnicity in Mauritius[45]. While Kreol is spoken by 54 % of the population there according to official statistics, many Indo-Mauritians in particular are unwilling to admit that Kreol is in fact their mother tongue because the language is also that of the Creole or Métis ethnic group. It was partly because of this ethnic association that the attempt to make Kreol the (supra-ethnic) national language of Mauritius in 1982 had to be eventually abandoned.

Considering that all modern states have language policies, be they *de jure* or *de facto* in nature, some ethnic (or national) groups are necessarily favored over others, a fact which has provoked much debate in discussions of liberalism, nationalism and democracy[46]. Just as choices

---

45. Thomas Hylland ERIKSEN, "Linguistic diversity and the quest for national identity : The case of Mauritius", *Ethnic and Racial Studies*, vol. 13, n° 1, 1990, p. 1-24.

46. See, for example, Brian WALKER, B. 1999. "Modernity and cultural vulnerability : should ethnicity be privileged ?", in Ronald BEINER [ed.], *Theorizing Nationalism*, Albany, State

concerning the official language in other contexts cannot be ethnoculturally neutral, the decision to make French the official language of Québec is no more civic than had another language been chosen. To echo the words of Fernand Dumont about the republican aspirations of the Patriot movement in 1837-38, French "is no more democratic in its essence than other languages[47]". Nonetheless, the idea of a completely ethnically neutral French seems to dominate contemporary Québec language policy. Indeed, the Larose report says absolutely nothing about the place of the majority group in the proposed new language policy, the Commission preferring to avoid all mention of ethnicity, no doubt because of the negative connotations of this term[48]. But the position defended is thereby made problematic : not only can it be

University of New York Press, 1999, p. 154 and Charles TAYLOR, "Nationalism and Modernity", in Robert McKIM and Jeff McMAHAN [eds.], *The Morality of Nationalism*, New York, Oxford University Press, 1997, p. 34.

47. Fernand DUMONT, *Genèse de la société québécoise*, Montréal, Boréal, 1993, p. 175.

48. See Guy BOUTHILLIER, *op. cit.*, p. 161.

considered disingenuous, it is also unwise, because it risks alienating Quebecers of French Canadian origin, who could then withdraw into themselves and adopt a defensive position with regard to French. One could not wish for a less desirable outcome, considering the efforts to promote French as a "language for everyone".

Paradoxically, the choice of the civic terms *langue publique commune* and *langue officielle* to refer to French in Québec also shows that language cannot be completely "de-ethnicized". If the new approach to Québécois identity defines the nation and all that is national as predominantly civic, why not refer to French as the "*langue nationale*", in the same way that Québec City is considered as the "*capitale nationale*", the library as the "*bibliothèque nationale*", and June 24th as the "*fête nationale*" of all Quebecers ? The answer lies almost certainly in that, more so than other symbols of identity, language is inextricably linked to ethnicity. Referring to French as the "*langue nationale*" would risk being considered as favoring the language of the ethnic majority.

In later versions of his model of the Québécois nation as a North American francophonie, Bouchard reduces the "ethnicity coefficient" to language alone, which he considers as an "indispensable vector to collective life[49]". In this way, he recognizes that language cannot be completely "de-ethnicized" as a matter of principal, making his approach one of the most viable among the many civic models currently proposed. In the particular case of Québec, the link between language and ethnicity is all the more inextricable because, since the secularization of society following the Quiet Revolution, it was language, together with the Québécois state, which came to replace the Church as the main bearer of French Canadian identity. Moreover, the relationship between language and ethnicity is mutually reinforcing : not only does the French language carry the French Canadian culture, French Canadian ethnicity is one of the major driving forces for the

---

49. Gérard BOUCHARD, *La nation québécoise au futur et au passé*, p. 64, 71.

maintenance of French language in North America. Yet this fact is completely ignored by many of the models proposed for Québec that are strictly civic.

> *Civic approaches like Bariteau's are void of underlying motivation if they cannot be understood as being motivated by the desire to ensure the survival of a common public culture of French expression. Now, despite the warnings of Dumont and Bouchard, new conceptions of the "Québécois nation" seem to want to keep this motivation which drives them in the dark. They believe that, simply by underlining in passing that French will be the language of citizenship of the new sovereign state, they can solve the problem of the survival of the French language in the few acres of snow lost in America, as well as the linguistic quarrels which arise on its territory. These positions are either naive or dishonest*[50].

50. Frédérick-Guillaume DUFOUR, *Patriotisme constitutionnel et nationalisme. Sur Jürgen Habermas,* Montréal, Liber, 2001, p. 198.

In other words, quite apart from the fact that language cannot be completely "de-ethnicized" as a matter of principle, one should not attempt to do so either. Ethnicity provides a necessary motivation for the survival of French, which reference to civic principles alone cannot inspire.

MOTIVATING NEW QUEBECERS

The issue of motivation is also important if new Quebecers are ever to be successfully encouraged to adopt French as a language of public communications. Much has been made of the claim that the only difference between the civic nation being proposed in Québec, and that which supposedly already exists in the United States, is that the "common public culture" into which immigrants are expected to integrate is not English but French-speaking[51]. Yet as far as the motiva-

---

51. Dominique AREL, "Political stability in multinational democracies : comparing language dynamics in Brussels, Montreal and Barcelona", in Alain-G. GAGNON and James TULLY [eds.], *Multinational Democracies,* Cambridge, Cambridge University Press, 2001, p. 75.

tions for second language acquisition are concerned, it is unwise to compare French and English in these two contexts when the languages do not enjoy the same power of attraction. Linguists generally identify two types of motivation underlying second language acquisition : instrumental and integrative or sentimental.

> *The first assumes that individuals are interested solely in acquiring sufficient communicative ability to satisfy their own specific goals, usually economic targets, while the second is based on the desire of individuals to associate themselves ever more closely with a target community to the point, eventually, of assimilating to it*[52].

In the North American context, studies have shown that instrumentalism is generally the primary motive behind the desire to immigrate to

---

52. Dennis AGER, *Motivation in Language Planning and Language Policy*, Clevedon, Multilingual Matters, 2001, p. 109.

the USA[53]. Moreover, regarding language, instrumental motivations extend beyond the borders of the US. Learning English will improve one's employment prospects anywhere on the North American continent or indeed in the world. By contrast, French in Québec cannot benefit from this degree of instrumental motivation : it is not the dominant language of the Canadian state, it is only spoken by 2 % of North America's population and has far fewer speakers than English world-wide. Despite important successes regarding French status language planning in Québec, it is generally accepted today that language legislation alone is not enough to guarantee the survival of French in North America. One of the areas recognized as also being important is immigration policy. Marc Levine identifies in particular the need for efficient mechanisms for welcoming and including immigrants, such as the promotion of a common French-speaking public culture to which immigrants feel they can both relate and

53. *Ibid.*, p. 114.

contribute[54]. In other words, there is a recognized need for integrative or sentimental motivations specific to Québec to supplement or reinforce the instrumental ones created by language legislation.

Aware of this need, the Québécois authorities there have made the promotion of integrative motivations amongst those of non-French Canadian descent one of their main strategies[55]. Indeed, the *Comité interministériel sur la situation de la langue française* explained in 1996 that "this expression 'langue commune' evokes the dual idea of 'communication' and of 'community'[56]". This stresses two important functions of French, even for new Quebecers. For even if French is a second language instead of a mother tongue for the latter, at least for the first generation, it does not follow that the attachment to this language must be

54. Marc Levine, *La reconquête de Montréal*, p. 385.

55. Ines Molinaro, "Contexte et intégration. Les communautés allophones au Québec", *Globe. Revue internationale d'études québécoises*, vol. 2, n° 2, 1999, p. 124.

56. Gouvernement du Québec, *Le français langue commune. Enjeu de la société québécoise*, p. 239.

purely instrumental : "second languages can play a significant role in one's linguistic identity[57]." To facilitate this type of identity function among new Quebecers, what is needed is not a new civic model of the Québec nation, but rather a so-called "integrationist[58]" model which, within an overall civic framework, nevertheless recognizes different ethnic identities and their various ways of relating to French.

As a first step in this direction, and to explain to immigrants that "in strictly linguistic terms, arriving in Québec is not equivalent to arriving in Canada[59]", the Larose Commission took up an idea introduced by the *Forum national sur la citoyenneté et l'intégration*[60] in 2000, by proposing

---

57. John JOSEPH, *Language and Identity : National, Ethnic, Religious*, Basingstoke, Palgrave Macmillan, 2004, p. 185.

58. Michel PAGÉ, "Propositions pour une approche dynamique de la situation du français dans l'espace linguistique québécois", forthcoming.

59. GOUVERNEMENT DU QUÉBEC, *Le français, une langue pour tout le monde*, p. 19.

60. GOUVERNEMENT DU QUÉBEC, *La citoyenneté québécoise. Document de consultation pour le forum national sur la*

the formalization of a Québécois citizenship to supplement, rather than replace, Canadian citizenship[61]. This idea was hotly debated, then rejected by the Minister concerned, Joseph Facal, on supposedly legal grounds. This article is not the place for an in-depth treatment of the notion of citizenship in general, or of what form it might take in the particular case of Québec. Suffice it to say here that the Commission was not referring to "nationality", which is often confused with "citizenship", especially in English[62]. Nor did it intend

citoyenneté et l'intégration, Québec, Ministère des Relations avec les citoyens et de l'Immigration, 2000.

61. GOUVERNEMENT DU QUÉBEC, *Le français, une langue pour tout le monde*, p. 21. On this proposal, see also Alain-G. GAGNON, "Plaidoyer pour une commission nationale sur la citoyenneté québécoise", *Le Devoir*, 15 June 2001, http://www.vigile.net/dossier-nation/1-6/15-gagnon.html (January 23rd 2003). On the more general references that the Québec authorities have made to citizenship since the 1990s, see Danielle JUTEAU, "The citizen makes an entrée : Redefining the national community in Quebec", *Citizenship Studies*, vol. 6, n° 4, 2002.

62. Historically and conceptually, there is an important distinction between nationality and citizenship. While the

"a citizenship in the sole legal capacity to participate in the exercise of power, but in the broader sense of belonging to a living heritage, founded on the sharing of common political and cultural references and on a shared identity[63]." As far as language policy is concerned, it is precisely this sort of measure which is required to create the integrative attachment to Québec needed if the notion of French as the *langue publique commune* for all Quebecers is to ever prove viable.

Denis Monière claims that "[t]he motivation for adopting French is necessarily weak and transitory among immigrants in a country which is officially bilingual and where English is the

---

former pertains to the international sphere, denoting "the link between a person and a state which guarantees him or her diplomatic protection", the latter refers to "a person's legal capacity to participate in the exercise of power by way of the right to vote and eligibility for public office" (GOUVERNEMENT DU QUÉBEC, *La citoyenneté québécoise. Document de consultation pour le forum national sur la citoyenneté et l'intégration*, p. 13-14).

63. GOUVERNEMENT DU QUÉBEC, *Le français, une langue pour tout le monde*, p. 12.

language of economic and social success[64]." In a similar manner, Bouchard goes as far as to say that sovereignty is a necessary condition for the successful implementation of his model of the Québécois nation built around French as the common denominator[65]. This may eventually prove so in the long term, but in the short term, an alternative could be found in a multidimensional citizenship, such as that which exists in the European Union. If a form could be found which was acceptable especially to Québec's English-speaking community, whose primary allegiance is to Canada, a Québécois citizenship could offer a means of including in the national project the segment of Québec population on which its renewal depends, namely Quebecers of immigrant descent[66].

---

64. Denis MONIÈRE, "La lutte des langues au Canada", *L'Action nationale,* vol. 93, n° 2, 2003, p. 23-24.

65. Gérard BOUCHARD, "Construire la nation québécoise. Manifeste pour une coalition nationale", p. 67-68.

66. The question of First Nations is even more complex, since many of these have little allegiance to Canada, not to mention Québec.

CONCLUSION

As this article has shown, language is not merely a means of communication; as a matter of principle, it cannot be completely "de-ethnicized". Moreover, in the particular case of Québec, it is not desirable to do so either. The new demographic reality brought about by immigration has understandably made it necessary to redefine the nation in more inclusive terms. But the introduction of a civic dimension should not entail the rejection of the identity of the ethnic core, which serves as an essential motivation for the maintenance of French. Any language policy which aims to promote French in Québec but which does not acknowledge that the language is also an important symbol of French Canadian identity thus seems doomed to failure.

That said, the survival of French in Québec also rests on its adoption by new Quebecers as their *lingua franca* for public communications. If the notion of French as a *langue publique commune* is to prove viable, additional sources of motivation need to be encouraged among new Quebecers in order to reinforce those resulting from language legislation, motivations that are of an integrative or sentimental nature and which are specific to Québec. Time may show that independence is the only sure way of creating the necessary conditions. However, in the meantime, it would be worthwhile seriously considering other possibilities, such as a new "integrationist" model of nation which, within an overall civic framework, recognizes the various ethnic identities of all Quebecers, including that of the majority group, as well as their different ways of relating to French. Conceived in a way which is acceptable to all Quebecers, a Québécois citizenship could constitute the basis of this new model, thereby providing an original strategy for guaranteeing the survival of French in North America.

SELECTED BIBLIOGRAPHY
ON THE LANGUAGE ISSUE IN QUÉBEC

AMYOT, Michel and Gilles BIBEAU, eds. *Le statut culturel du français au Québec*. Québec City : Conseil de la langue française, 1984.

BEAUDET, Marie-Andrée. *Langue et littérature au Québec (1895-1914)*. Montréal : L'Hexagone, 1991.

BELLEAU, Irène and Gilles DORION, eds. *Les œuvres de création et le français au Québec*. Québec City : Conseil de la langue française and Service des communications, 1984.

BOUCHARD, Chantal. *La langue et le nombril. Histoire d'une obsession québécoise*. Montréal : Fides, 2002.

BOUTHILLIER, Guy and Jean MEYNAUD, eds. *Le choc des langues au Québec 1760-1960*. 2nd edition. Montréal : Presses de l'Université du Québec, 1972.

CALDWELL, Gary and W. WADDELL. *The English of Quebec*. Québec City : Institut québécois de recherche sur la culture, 1982.

COMBRES, Alain. "La question linguistique et les partis politiques québécois (1960-1990)". Paris, Université de Paris I, Panthéon-Sorbonne, Ph.D. dissertation, 1996.

CORBEIL, Jean-Claude. "Essai sur l'origine historique de la situation linguistique du Québec" [1974]. In *Le français hors de France*. Edited by Albert Valdman. Paris : Champion, 1979, p. 21-31.

CORBEIL, Jean-Claude. *L'aménagement linguistique du Québec*. Montréal : Guérin, 1980.

CORBEIL, Jean-Claude. *Langue et usages des langues*. Québec City : Conseil de la langue française, 1986.

CORBETT, Noël, ed. *Langue et identité. Le français et les francophones d'Amérique du Nord*. Québec City : Presses de l'Université Laval, 1990.

COULOMBE, Pierre. *Language Rights in French Canada*. New York : Peter Lang Publishing, 1995.

DAOUST, Paul. "Les jugements sur le joual (1959-1975) à la lumière de la linguistique et de la sociolinguistique". Montréal : Université de Montréal, Ph.D. dissertation, 1983.

FARINA, Annick. *Dictionnaires de langue française du Canada. Lexicographie et société au Québec.* Paris : Honoré Champion, 2001.

GAUVIN, Lise. "L'épopée du joual", *Parti pris littéraire*. Montréal : Presses de l'Université de Montréal, 1975, p. 55-74.

GAUVIN, Lise. *Langagement. L'écrivain et la langue au Québec.* Montréal : Boréal, 2000.

GÉMAR, Jean-Claude. *Les trois états de la politique linguistique du Québec, d'une société traduite à une société d'expression.* Québec City : Conseil de la langue française, Service des communications, 1983.

GERVAIS, André, ed. *Emblématiques de l'époque du joual : Jacques Renaud, Gérald Godin, Michel Tremblay, Yvon Deschamps.* Outremont : Lanctôt, 2000.

GODIN, Pierre. *La poudrière linguistique.* Montréal : Boréal, 1990.

GRUTMAN, Rainier. *Des langues qui résonnent. L'hétérolinguisme au XIXe siècle québécois.* Montréal : Fides, 1997.

LAROSE, Karim. *La langue de papier. Spéculations linguistiques au Québec (1957-1977)*. Montréal : Presses de l'Université de Montréal, 2004.

LAURIN, Camille. *Le français, langue du Québec*. Montréal : Éditions du Jour, 1977.

LECLERC, Jacques, with the collaboration of Lionel JEAN. "La question linguistique au Québec", *Langue et société*. Laval : Mondia, 1992, p. 605-650.

LEVINE, Marc V. *La reconquête de* Montréal. Translated from English by Marie Poirier. Montréal : VLB, 1997.

LOCKERBIE, Ian. "Le débat sur l'aménagement du français au Québec." *Globe. Revue internationale d'études québécoises*, vol. 6, n° 1, 2003, p. 125-149.

MARTEL, Pierre and Hélène CAJOLET-LAGANIÈRE. *La qualité de la langue au Québec*. Québec City : Institut québécois de recherche sur la culture, 1995.

MARTEL, Pierre and Hélène CAJOLET-LAGANIÈRE. *Le français québécois. Usages, standard et aménagement*. Québec City : Institut québécois de recherche sur la culture, 1996.

Maurais, Jacques. "La crise du français au Québec." In *La crise des langues*. Edited by Jacques Maurais. Québec City : Conseil de la langue française and Paris : Le Robert, 1985, p. 39-83.

Maurais, Jacques. *Les langues autochtones du Québec*. Québec City : Les Publications du Québec, 1992.

Maurais, Jacques and Édith Bédard. "Réflexions sur la normalisation linguistique au Québec." In *La norme linguistique*. Edited by Jacques Maurais and Édith Bédard. Québec City : Conseil de la langue française and Paris : Le Robert, 1983, p. 435-459.

Mercier, Louis. *La Société du parler français au Canada et la mise en valeur du patrimoine linguistique québécois (1902-1962). Histoire de son enquête et genèse de son glossaire*. Québec City : Les Presses de l'Université Laval, 2002.

Noël, Danièle. *Les questions de langue au Québec (1759-1850)*. Québec City : Conseil de la langue française, 1990.

Plourde, Michel. *La langue française au Québec. Conférences et allocutions (1980-1985)*. Québec City : Éditeur officiel du Québec and Conseil de la langue française, 1985.

PLOURDE, Michel. *La politique linguistique du Québec (1977-1987)*. Québec City : Institut québécois de recherche, 1988.

PLOURDE, Michel, ed., with the collaboration of Hélène DUVAL and Pierre GEORGEAULT. *Le français au Québec. 400 ans d'histoire et de* vie. Québec City : Conseil de la langue française, 2000.

POIRIER, Claude, ed., with the collaboration of Aurélien BOIVIN, Cécyle TRÉPANIER and Claude VERREAULT. *Langue, espace, société. Les variétés du français en Amérique du Nord*. Sainte-Foy : Presses de l'Université Laval, 1994.

ABOUT THE AUTHORS

Karim LAROSE teaches literature and is a postdoctoral researcher with the Département des littératures, Université Laval. His research efforts are focused on the Québec language issue, Québec poetry and non-fictional prose, as well as the problematics of marginal or minor literatures. He has published a comprehensive work titled *La langue de papier. Spéculations linguistiques au Québec (1957-1977)* (Montréal, 2004), a revised and enlarged version of his doctoral thesis, which won the Académie des Grands Montréalais award of excellence in 2004.

Ian LOCKERBIE is Emeritus Professor of French at the University of Stirling, Scotland. He is the author of numerous articles on Québec literature, theatre and cinema, and the editor of a volume on theatre and cinema in Québec and Scotland. He was adviser on

Québec for the *New Oxford Companion to Literature in French* (Oxford, 1995) and for *Francophone Studies: The Essential Glossary* (London, 2002). He was the first recipient of the Prix du Québec in the UK, awarded for research on Québec themes.

Ines MOLINARO is Director of the Liberal Arts Programme and Coordinator of Senior Courses at St Clare's, Oxford. Born in Montréal, she earned her postgraduate degrees in politics at the University of Notre Dame (Indiana) and taught political science at the Universities of Birmingham, Warwick and Cambridge (1996-2003). In Cambridge, she was the Fellow in Canadian Studies in the Faculty of Social and Political Sciences (SPS), and the Director of Studies for SPS at Gonville and Caius College and Lucy Cavendish College.

Leigh OAKES is a professor of French at Queen Mary, University of London. His research explores questions of national identity and language in Québec, Sweden, France and the European Union. He has published *Language and National Identity: Comparing France and Sweden* (Amsterdam, 2001), as well as several articles in periodicals such as the *Journal of Multilingual and*

Multicultural Development, the *Journal of French Language Studies* and *Nations and Nationalism.* He is currently involved in a project dealing with questions of language, citizenship and identity within the framework of new civic conceptions of the nation.

NEW PERSPECTIVES IN QUÉBEC STUDIES

PRINTED
FOR ÉDITIONS NOTA BENE
IN CAP-SAINT-IGNACE, QUÉBEC
BY MARQUIS
IMPRIMEUR INC.
IN MAY 2005

Legal deposit, 2nd quarter 2005
Bibliothèque nationale du Québec